Cost–Benefit Analysis of Proposed California Oil and Gas Refinery Regulations

Daniel Gonzales, Timothy R. Gulden, Aaron Strong, William Hoyle

T0308369

For more information on this publication, visit www.rand.org/t/RR1421

Library of Congress Cataloging-in-Publication Data is available for this publication.
ISBN: 978-0-8330-9412-4

Published by the RAND Corporation, Santa Monica, Calif.

© Copyright 2016 RAND Corporation

RAND® is a registered trademark.

Cover image: Shell Martinez refinery in Contra Costa County, California (via Contra Costa Hazardous Materials Programs)

Support RAND

Make a tax-deductible charitable contribution at
www.rand.org/giving/contribute

www.rand.org

Preface

The state of California has proposed revised process safety management (PSM) and California Accidental Release Prevention regulations for oil and gas refineries that operate in California. The proposed regulations are more stringent than current federal regulations and are intended to improve refinery-worker and public safety and reduce air pollution.

The objective of this study was to assess the costs and benefits of the proposed California PSM and California Accidental Release Prevention regulations. We estimate these costs and benefits in four categories: the costs to industry (to implement the regulation), the costs to society (pass-through of certain industry costs), benefits to industry, and benefits to society.

This study examined the PSM activities called for in the proposed regulation. Many, if not all, of these costs will likely be passed on to California consumers in the form of higher prices for petroleum products. However, the new PSM regulations could improve safety at California refineries, which would, in turn, result in fewer major process incidents and fewer releases of hazardous materials from refineries. Because the number of major refinery incidents (MRIs) might decline under the proposed regulation, the regulation could provide safety and health benefits to the public in nearby communities and might provide other economic benefits. We examined these potential benefits in this study. This report explains the proposed regulations, describes our methodology, and offers our findings and recommendations.

Christine Baker, director of the California Department of Industrial Relations, and Alice Busching Reynolds, deputy secretary for law enforcement and counsel of the California Environmental Protection Agency, sponsored the research reported here. Under its Division of Occupational Safety and Health, the California Department of Industrial Relations operates a PSM unit, which enforces the California PSM standard (Cal. Code Regs. tit. 8, § 5189) and will be charged with enforcing the new proposed PSM standard for refineries, § 5189.1.

Infrastructure Resilience and Environmental Policy

The research reported here was conducted in the RAND Infrastructure Resilience and Environmental Policy Program, which conducts analyses on urbanization and other stresses. This includes research on infrastructure development, infrastructure financing, energy policy, urban planning and the role of public–private partnerships, transportation policy, climate response, mitigation and adaption, environmental sustainability, and water resources management and coastal protection. Program research is supported by government agencies, foundations, and the private sector.

This program is part of RAND Justice, Infrastructure, and Environment, a division of the RAND Corporation dedicated to improving policy and decisionmaking in a wide range of policy domains, including civil and criminal justice, infrastructure protection and homeland security, transportation and energy policy, and environmental and natural resource policy.

Questions or comments about this report should be sent to the project leader, Daniel Gonzales (Daniel_Gonzales@rand.org). For more information about the RAND Infrastructure Resilience and Environmental Policy Program, see http://www.rand.org/jie or contact the director at irep@rand.org.

Contents

Figures and Tables

Figures

Tables

Summary

A revision to process safety management (PSM) and California Accidental Release Prevention regulations has been drafted that incorporates recommendations of the final report of the governor's Interagency Working Group on Refinery Safety and key elements of the Contra Costa County industrial safety ordinance (ISO). The proposed refinery PSM standard represents a significant change from the existing PSM standard contained in Title 8, Section 5189. It includes new management system elements, a more carefully defined hazard analysis process, and provisions to expand employee participation and employee access to reports and other information developed pursuant to the standard. It also requires damage mechanism reviews for each process used in refinery operations and a hierarchy-of-hazard-control analysis for a wide range of refinery operations, planning, and engineering. This regulatory approach has some similarity to the regulations that have been put into successful practice in the United Kingdom and Norway.

These new California regulations will likely increase refinery planning and other costs, but they might also benefit refinery workers and the public by reducing the rate of serious refinery incidents, workplace injuries, and accidental discharges of hazardous and toxic substances to the atmosphere.

Objective

The objective of this study was to assess the costs and benefits of the proposed California PSM and California Accidental Release Prevention regulations that are designed to improve the safety of oil and gas refineries operating in the state of California.

These costs and benefits fall into four categories:

- costs to industry (to implement the regulation)
- costs to society (a pass-through of certain industry costs)
- benefits to industry (costs avoided)
- benefits to society (costs avoided and other improvements and fewer worker deaths).

Once we have estimated these subcategories of costs and benefits, we integrate them into a consistent portrait of costs and benefits to the California economy using a widely used macroeconomic model. This provides a systematic way of avoiding double counting while capturing many of the secondary economic effects that result from changes in prices, employment, and related impacts of the regulations.

Costs to Industry

We engaged process safety and cost experts at each refinery in California to develop comprehensive estimates of the costs to implement all aspects of the proposed regulation. We provide the details of these cost estimates in Chapter Four and summarize them below. We calculate costs in 12 major areas that the regulations cover: safety training, damage mechanism reviews, root-cause analysis, hierarchy-of-hazard-control analysis, process safety culture assessment, program management, performance indicators, human factors, safeguard protection analysis (SPA), layer-of-protection analysis (LOPA), process hazard analysis, and other (or undifferentiated) costs. We base these estimates on detailed answers that refiners provided for a set of structured interview questions designed as part of the study to elicit the expected marginal costs of the proposed regulations for various aspects of PSM.

It is important to note that there were significant differences in the size and composition of the proprietary cost estimates that we received from the 12 refiners that operate in the state. We employed several cost-aggregation techniques to handle these differences and to account for capacity differences between refineries. Summing costs from all refiners produced a best estimate of $58 million per year for refiners to maintain compliance with the proposed regulations.

We used the variance in cost estimates from one refiner to the next as a way of assessing and quantifying the uncertainty in the estimates. These uncertainties include both incomplete knowledge of what it will cost to meet well-understood objectives and, in cases in which one could interpret the regulatory language in multiple ways, unknown aspects of regulatory implementation. Refiners surveyed expressed a wide range of opinions about the degree to which the new regulations might differ in practice from existing regulations, and the range of costs estimated reflects these interpretations. Using the aggregation techniques described in Chapter Four to quantify this uncertainty, we calculate a range of $20 million per year on the low end and $183 million per year on the high end.

The one area of significant disagreement in the refiner cost estimates was regarding start-up costs. Most refiners estimated start-up costs for the first one to five years to be on the same order as, or lower than, ongoing costs. One refining company, however, expressed concern about the costs to comply with SPA and LOPA provisions of the proposed regulation. If this refiner's assessment of the proposed regulation is correct, costs in the first five years could be 20 times as high as our estimate of ongoing costs. It should be noted that we did not include these SPA and LOPA start-up costs in the core cost estimates presented in Table S.1. Informed by our own independent review of the proposed regulation and associated near-term SPA and LOPA implementation requirements, we conclude that the other California refiners properly interpreted the proposed regulation.

Costs to Society

We have estimated the price impact of the proposed regulations under the assumptions that additional regulatory costs will be passed on to consumers through increased gasoline prices and that demand for gasoline is perfectly inelastic. In recent years, gasoline consumption in California has averaged about 14.5 billion gallons per year.

California requires a unique reformulated gasoline blend to meet the state's pollution-control requirements. Gasoline made in other states to meet other state and federal pollution-control requirements does not meet California standards. Consequently, all gasoline consumed in California is typically made in the state.[1] Therefore, California refiners' costs to implement the proposed regulations can be distributed over consumers' costs to purchase 14.5 billion gallons of California gasoline.

Spreading the $58 million estimated cost of the regulations across this volume of sales indicates an increase in price of about $0.004 per gallon. The lower estimate of $20 million moves this impact down to $0.0014, while the upper estimate of $183 million moves the impact up to $0.013 per gallon.

Aggregating this to calculate the impact on the average adult Californian gives an estimated cost per person of about $2 per year, with a low estimate of $0.68 and a high estimate of $6.20 per person per year.

The larger economic impacts of this cost on the California economy are mixed. After applying these costs to a standard input–output model of the state, we find that

Table S.1
Estimated Marginal Cost of Regulatory Compliance, in Dollars

Estimate	Amount
Refiner-estimated total	57,571,983
Low	19,589,755
High	183,420,000

---

[1]   Only one known exception to this observation had reportedly occurred in the past decade up until June 2015. We examine details of this episode in the body of this report.

the additional refiner spending on labor drives higher costs and more than offsets the drag that this slightly higher cost of gasoline places on the economy. On net, we conclude, the stimulatory effect of the refiners' additional spending would slightly exceed the inhibitory effect of higher gas prices.

Benefits to Industry: Safety Improvements

Safety improvements could result from implementing the proposed regulation. These safety improvements could reduce the number of major refinery incidents (MRIs) at California refineries. We estimated the proposed regulations' possible safety impact by using the Contra Costa County ISO as a proxy for the proposed regulations. The Contra Costa County ISO is a more stringent regulation than the current California or federal standards and contains some of the key elements of the proposed refinery regulations. The proposed regulations build on the ISO requirement, requiring state-of-the-art PSM practices that are designed to provide greater levels of reliability and safety than the Contra Costa County ISO currently provides, so the proposed regulations will likely be more stringent than the current Contra Costa County ISO. Therefore, it is not unreasonable to assume that California refinery-incident rates under the proposed regulation will be similar to or lower than those of ISO refineries. The hypothesis we examine is whether refiners that implement the measures called for in the proposed regulation would suffer fewer major incidents and thereby avoid many of the ensuing costs. The ISO and non-ISO (NISO) refinery-incident history analysis presented in this report provides evidence to support this hypothesis. In this analysis, we showed that the incident rate for major incidents was significantly less for ISO refineries than for NISO refineries operating in the state of California. We present details of this analysis in Chapter Five.

We found no evidence, however, that the proposed regulations would reduce the long-term operating costs of California refineries.

Benefits to Industry: Costs Avoided

Safety improvements could result from implementing the proposed regulation. These safety improvements could reduce the number of costly MRIs (CMRIs). Therefore, a benefit to industry of the proposed regulation is that the costs of major incidents could be reduced in the future. In the study, we estimated the costs of a costly major incident for a California refinery (an incident that has a macroeconomic impact of greater than $1.5 billion on the California economy). At least three refinery incidents of this magnitude have occurred in California since 1999. Our analysis reveals that the average cost of such an incident to the refiner that suffers the incident is at least $220 million.

Caveats

The above estimate is only a lower bound of the total cost to the refiner suffering an outage caused by a major incident. We could not reliably estimate all refinery equipment repair, company reputation damage, overseas production costs for reformulated California gasoline, intermediate feedstock production and transportation costs, or gasoline transportation costs without access to detailed proprietary information that refiners were unwilling to share with us.[2]

Benefits to Society: Costs Avoided

In quantitative terms, the largest potential benefit of the proposed regulations is the avoided cost of fuel supply disruption related to a future MRI. Our analysis of gasoline prices in California versus the rest of the United States in response to the 2015 incident at Exxon Mobil Corporation's Torrance Refinery indicated a cost to California drivers of nearly $2.4 billion, which took the form of a prolonged $0.40 increase in gasoline prices. Macroeconomic analysis indicates that the lost supply associated with this one incident reduced the size of the California economy by $6.9 billion.

The above costs to California consumers and the California economy assume a refinery outage of six months in duration. Press reports now indicate that the Exxon-Mobil Torrance Refinery outage could last up to 12 months. In this case, the costs to consumers and the California economy could double unless large quantities of gasoline are imported from overseas refineries.[3]

A reduction in the number of refinery incidents would enable Californians to avoid other costs that would be incurred by residents who live near the refinery afflicted by the incident. These include costs for

- emergency services
- health care
- reductions in property values
- reductions in local tax revenue to local governments.

---

[2] When we conducted this research, the ExxonMobil Torrance Refinery incident was ongoing. Discussions with the refiner indicated that ExxonMobil had not yet determined the full extent of the costs incurred as a result of the incident. Other refiners were unwilling to share any postincident refinery-repair costs with us.

[3] Some California refiners, in private communications, indicated that this was not economically feasible to do if the refinery outage was relatively short lived (of six months or less) given the unique manufacturing requirements for reformulated California gasoline.

Benefits to Society: Deaths Avoided

A reduction in the number of refinery incidents also would confer other noneconomic benefits on residents living near refineries. They would be less likely to be injured or die in such incidents. However, we could not quantify these noneconomic benefits in this study. And, of course, this important benefit would also be conferred on workers at California refineries. Our analysis of MRIs show that, in many such incidents, a refinery worker dies; in a few such incidents, multiple refinery workers die. If such events can be avoided, worker safety will be improved, and the number of workers who die will be reduced. In this study, we examined the hypothesis that the implementation of the proposed regulation will result in fewer refinery-worker deaths. We examine worker deaths in ISO and NISO refineries and find that these data provide evidence to support this hypothesis. In this analysis, we showed that the ISO refinery-worker death rate was substantially lower than that for NISO refineries operating in the state of California.

Balancing Costs and Benefits

To compare the costs and benefits of the regulations, we use a break-even analysis framework. The specific break-even analysis approach we employ has been used in terrorism risk modeling, but it can be applied to a broad set of cost–benefit problems (Willis and LaTourrette, 2008). As shown in Chapter Five, the incidents in 2015 at ExxonMobil's Torrance, in 2012 at the Chevron Refinery in Richmond, and in 1999 at Tosco Corporation's Avon Refinery in Martinez appear to be the costliest major incidents that have occurred in California in the past 16 years and those for which reasonably accurate economic data are available. As explained in Chapter Five, less costly major incidents are more frequent than major incidents that result in major costs for California consumers, complicating an analysis of this sort. We focus on those very costly major incidents because they are responsible for the vast majority of the economic losses resulting from refinery incidents.

Because CMRIs in California are rare, the variance for this data set is large, which indicates significant uncertainty in the estimates for the expected annual loss from such events. In light of this uncertainty, we can generalize the analysis to account for a range of estimates for the true expected cost of major refinery incidents in the state of California. Figure S.1 shows the relationship between estimated preregulation annual expected loss from major refinery events and the critical risk reduction required to justify the expense of the proposed regulations. Larger expected annual loss assumptions require smaller reductions in risk in order for the benefits of regulation to offset the costs, while lower estimates of expected annual loss (caused, for example, by lower

Figure S.1
Critical Risk Reduction as a Function of Differing Estimates of
Preregulation Expected Annual Loss from Costly Major Refinery
Incidents

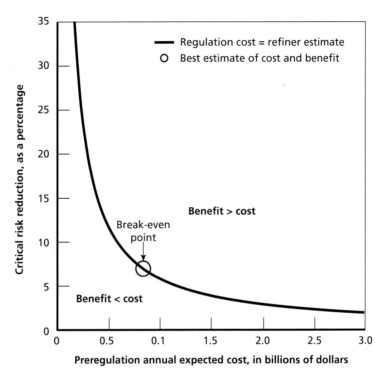

estimates of refinery incident frequency) must produce greater improvements in risk to be worthwhile.

In Figure S.1, the small circle indicates our best estimate for the break-even point, the point at which the annual cost of implementing the proposed regulation equals the expected annual loss from CMRIs. That is, given the expected annual loss of $800 million to the California economy (estimated in Chapter Seven) associated with CMRIs, the proposed regulations will have to reduce the risk from such incidents by 7.3 percent.

Figure S.2 shows the range of uncertainty associated with the critical risk-reduction factor. Table S.2 shows a small subset of possible points from the figure to illustrate how several key factors are related in these uncertainty calculations. Table S.2 shows that, assuming our best estimate of the expected annual loss, under the low estimate for the implementation costs of the proposed regulation given in Table S.1, risk must be reduced by only 2.5 percent, whereas, under the high estimate given in Table S.1, risk must be reduced by 22.9 percent to justify the cost of the regulations. If one assumes an expected annual loss from costly major refinery incidents of only

Figure S.2
Effect That Uncertainty About Regulation Cost Has on Critical Risk-Reduction Value

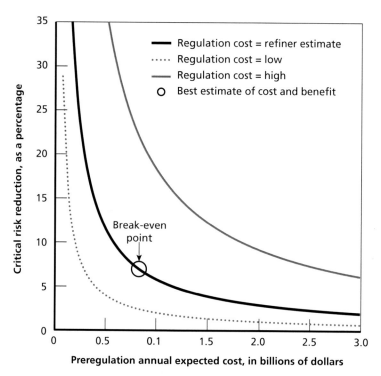

RAND RR1421-S.2

Table S.2
Critical Risk-Reduction Values for Various Assumptions Regarding Expected Annual Loss and Regulation Cost

Expected Annual Loss, in Millions of Dollars	Critical Risk Reduction, as a Percentage		
	Low Estimate of Implementation Costs	Refiner-Estimated Implementation Costs	High Estimate of Implementation Costs
200	10.0	29.0	91.7
400	5.0	14.5	45.9
800[a]	2.5	7.3[b]	22.9
1,200	1.7	4.8	15.3
1,600	1.3	3.6	11.5

[a] Best estimate of expected annual loss.

[b] Best estimate of break-even point.

$400 million, these critical risk-reduction values rise, with the refiner-estimated costs requiring a reduction of 14.5 percent, the low-cost scenario 5 percent, and the high-cost scenario 45.9 percent. If, on the other hand, one assumes an expected annual cost of $1.2 billion, the critical risk-reduction values are 4.8 percent in the refiner-estimated case (our best estimate for regulation implementation costs), 1.7 percent in the low-cost case, and 15.3 percent in the high-cost case.

Our analysis of ISO versus NISO refineries supports the idea that more-stringent regulation can produce real gains in refinery safety. To the extent that the proposed regulations resemble the Contra Costa County ISO, we might expect similar improvements. To the extent that the proposed regulations go beyond the ISO, they might be expected to produce greater safety gains—though various differences in the structure and implementation of the two regulatory regimes make precise quantitative comparison difficult.

Under most scenarios examined in this analysis, the regulations appear to be cost-effective. The various cells in Table S.2 do not have equal probability. Our best estimate for expected loss from MRIs is $800 million per year, and our best estimate for the cost of the regulations (developed from refiner surveys) is $58 million per year. These most likely estimates require the regulations to reduce risk by 7.3 percent in order to be economically justified. This seems quite attainable given the success of the Contra Costa County ISO. If annual losses are actually lower, or if the cost of the regulations will actually be higher, the case for the regulations is less strong. In particular, if the annual losses are in the range of $200 million per year (one-quarter of what we have estimated), the critical risk reduction approaches 30 percent under the refiner-estimated cost scenario. Similarly, if regulatory implementation costs resemble the high end of the refiner estimates, the required risk reductions climb to more than 25 percent if annual losses are anything less than what we have estimated.

On the other hand, most of the refiner-estimated cost scenarios appear justifiable. If annual losses are more than half of what we have estimated (more than $400 million per year), risk reductions of less than 15 percent are required to justify the regulations. Similarly, if the costs of implementation are closer to the low end of the refiner estimates, no plausible expected loss scenario requires a risk reduction of more than 10 percent. Even under the high-cost scenario, expected losses at or above our best estimate of $800 million per year require risk reductions of less than 25 percent. Reductions of this magnitude seem quite plausible given the history of the Contra Costa County ISO.

Our estimate for expected annual losses is conservative. We omit losses from all but the three most major recent incidents. Also, we have based our cost for the ExxonMobil incident on a shutdown time of six months. Estimates as of the time of publication are that the refinery could be off-line for a full 12 months. This could lead to a significant increase in the estimate for expected annual losses. If so, this would drive the critical risk-reduction levels downward, making the regulations more cost-effective.

Important Qualitative Factors

This analysis was able to capture and quantify most of the potential costs of the regulation but was less able to quantify other benefits, such as avoided injury, avoided environmental harm, and peace of mind for the residents of California. To the extent that this statement is true, the numbers presented here provide a conservative estimate of the benefits. This has the effect of lowering the required break-even point and making the regulations easier to justify.

Acknowledgments

We recognize California governor Edmund G. Brown, Jr., for his leadership and commitment to the health and safety of California refinery workers and surrounding communities. We are grateful to Clifford Rechtschaffen, senior adviser to the governor; David M. Lanier, secretary of the California Labor and Workforce Development Agency; and Matthew Rodriquez, California Secretary for Environmental Protection, California Environmental Protection Agency (CalEPA). We are also grateful to Christine Baker, director of the California Department of Industrial Relations (DIR); Gina Solomon, deputy secretary for science and health at CalEPA; Alice Busching Reynolds, deputy secretary for law enforcement and counsel at CalEPA; and Mark S. Ghilarducci, director of the California Governor's Office of Emergency Services for their insights and guidance at a formative stage of this research.

Juliann Sum, chief of the Division of Occupational Safety and Health; Clyde Trombettas; Amy R. Coombe; Kumani Louis Armstrong; Amy Martin; Michael P. Wilson; and Sean Ahearn, also from DIR, provided our study team with key pieces of information and shared their insights with us on the intent of the proposed regulations. We thank these key staff members at DIR for their help and support.

We are also grateful to Floyd Vergara, Emily Wimberger, and Chantel Crane of the California Air Resources Board. They provided guidance and background information important for this study.

We thank Randall L. Sawyer, director of Contra Costa County Health Services Hazardous Materials Programs, for his invaluable help with this study. Randy described the history of refinery incidents in Contra Costa County, the impetus for the Contra Costa County industrial safety ordinance (ISO), and the key features of the ISO to the RAND study team.

We thank and also met with workers' union representatives who provided their own perspectives on the proposed regulations and on refinery safety.

We thank Robbie Hunter and Cesar Diaz of the State Building and Construction Trades Council for their input and support.

We thank the following people for their help: Mike Wright, Kim Nibarger, Michael Smith, Steven P. Sullivan, Tracy W. Scott, Ron Espinoza, and David Campbell of United Steelworkers.

A variety of oil and gas refinery business, cost, and process safety managers provided critical cost information to us and shared their concerns and insights on the proposed regulation. We are grateful to the following people for their contributions to this study:

- Teresa K. Makarewicz, manager, California Business Coordination for Shell Oil Products U.S.
- Mary Kay Nye, manager, process safety, Shell Oil Products U.S. Martinez Refinery
- James Jeter, senior manager, environmental, health, and safety, Tesoro Refining and Marketing
- Sabiha Gokcen, manager, process safety, Tesoro Golden Eagle Refinery
- Rod Spackman, manager, policy, government, and public affairs, Los Angeles Basin, Chevron Corporation
- Chris Larsen, manager, process safety, Chevron El Segundo Refinery, Chevron Corporation
- Karen Tancredi, process safety, Chevron El Segundo Refinery, Chevron Corporation
- Tery Lizarraga, manager, process safety, Chevron Richmond Refinery, Chevron Corporation
- Robert Young, senior safety supervisor, Torrance Refinery, Exxon Mobil Corporation
- David Ingram, manager, safety, security, health, and environment, Torrance Refinery, Exxon Mobil Corporation
- Linda Cohu, risk management, Los Angeles Refinery, Phillips 66
- Peter Schnieders, manager, technical services, Los Angeles Refinery, Phillips 66
- Mike Lee, manager, process safety, Los Angeles Refinery, Phillips 66
- Lawrence B. Silva, manager, health, safety, and environment, San Francisco Refinery facility at Rodeo, Phillips 66
- Steve Harms, superintendent, health and safety, San Francisco Refinery facility at Rodeo, Phillips 66 Rodeo
- Denis I. Kurt, senior manager, environment, health, and safety, Los Angeles refinery, Tesoro Refining and Marketing
- Jocelyn Ching, superintendent, process safety, Los Angeles refinery, Tesoro Refining and Marketing
- Matt Tyson, economics and planning, Los Angeles refinery, Tesoro Refining and Marketing

- Patrick Covert, executive regional director, environmental and regulatory services, Valero Companies
- Jason Lee, senior manager, health and safety, Valero Companies
- Michael Butler, manager, process safety, Valero Wilmington Refinery, Valero Marketing and Supply
- Wayne Howard, manager, process safety, Valero Benicia Refinery, Valero Marketing and Supply
- Melinda Hicks, manager, environmental health and safety, Kern Oil and Refining
- Bill Winters, senior vice president, human resources and community affairs, Paramount Petroleum
- Bill Little, general manager, Paramount Refinery
- Michael Vigliarolo, manager, process safety, Paramount Petroleum.

We thank Guy Bjerke and Thomas A. Umenhofer of the Western States Petroleum Association for assistance in reaching out to the Western States Petroleum Association membership regarding this study.

We met or corresponded with local and county officials whose offices serve as Certified Unified Program Agencies for refinery incidents in their jurisdictions. We are also grateful to the following people for their help:

- Anna Olekszyk, professional engineer, Risk Management and Prevention Program Specialist, City of Los Angeles Fire Department
- Martin A. Serna, fire chief, fire department, City of Torrance
- James Carver, fire marshal, El Segundo Fire Department
- Colby La Place, senior hazardous material specialist, Solano County Department of Resource Management.

Finally, we thank our peer reviewers, Henry H. Willis of RAND; Andrew Hopkins, emeritus professor of sociology, Australian National University; and Tom LaTourrette, director of quality assurance for RAND Justice, Infrastructure, and Environment. Their thoughtful reviews have made an immeasurable difference in quality, clarity, and correctness of this report.

Abbreviations

API	American Petroleum Institute
bpd	barrel per day
CalARP	California Accidental Release Prevention
CalEPA	California Environmental Protection Agency
Cal/OSHA	Division of Occupational Safety and Health
CCHMP	Contra Costa Hazardous Materials Programs
CGE	computable general equilibrium
CI	confidence interval
CMRI	costly major refinery incident
CSB	U.S. Chemical Safety and Hazard Investigation Board
CUPA	Certified Unified Program Agency
DIR	Department of Industrial Relations
DMR	damage mechanism review
ESP	electrostatic precipitator
GSP	gross state product
HCA	hierarchy-of-hazard-control analysis
HF	human factor
ISO	industrial safety ordinance
LOPA	layer-of-protection analysis
MCAR	major chemical accident or release

MI	mechanical integrity
MOOC	management of organizational change
MRI	major refinery incident
NDA	nondisclosure agreement
NISO	non–industrial safety ordinance
PHA	process hazard analysis
PI	performance indicator
PM	program management
PSCA	process safety culture assessment
PSE	process safety event
PSM	process safety management
RAGAGEP	recognized and generally accepted good engineering practices
RCA	root-cause analysis
RFG	reformulated gasoline
RFP	request for proposals
RMP	risk management plan
SB	Senate bill
SP	safety plan
SPA	safeguard protection analysis

CHAPTER ONE

Introduction

Background

California consumes a large amount of petroleum products. So, not surprisingly, the oil and gas refinery industry plays an important role in the California economy. The majority of refined products produced in California are consumed by cars and trucks driven in the state and by commercial aircraft refueled at the state's airports. In 2014, more than 23 million automobiles were registered in California (California Department of Motor Vehicles, 2015). If we include all types of motor vehicles, more than 33 million motor vehicles (including trucks) were registered in the state of California in 2014 (California Department of Motor Vehicles, 2015). Only 1.6 percent of the automobiles registered in the state of California in 2012 were electric vehicles (Caldwell, 2014). Even though the number of electric vehicles is increasing modestly over time, the majority of the vehicles on the road today in California use gasoline or diesel fuel.

California motor vehicles and commercial aircraft consumed 14.5 billion gallons of gasoline, diesel, and jet fuel in 2012. Gasoline consumption fell about 14 percent from 2006 to 2012 because of the increasing efficiency of motor vehicles, but it has remained steady, at about 14.5 billion gallons per year, over the past few years as economic conditions have improved and recently as oil prices have dropped. Consequently, the California oil and gas industry will remain important to the California economy for the foreseeable future.

California Gas Market

The California oil and gas market is isolated from the larger U.S. market for petroleum products because of California's unique pollution-control regulations. California requires the use of a unique blend of reformulated gasoline (RFG) to reduce airborne pollution and the potential for groundwater pollution (California Environmental Protection Agency [CalEPA], 2015). Two blends of California gasoline are used: one in summer and another in winter. Summer and winter RFG blends are produced and used in other parts of the country, but California pollution-control requirements are stricter than federal requirements (CalEPA, 2015). Consequently, most oil and gas refineries in the United States outside of California produce RFG blends that do not meet California requirements and so cannot be sold in California. There also are no pipelines from other major refinery states (e.g., Texas) to California, making it costly to import gasoline or other refined products from Gulf Coast refineries to California. For these reasons, almost all of the gasoline that California motor vehicles consume is refined within the state. Consequently, California refineries operate largely in their own market.

Proposed Refinery Regulations

Revised California process safety management (PSM) and California Accidental Release Prevention (CalARP) regulations have been proposed for oil and gas refineries that operate in the state. The proposed regulations are more stringent than current federal regulations and are intended to improve refinery-worker safety, improve public safety in nearby communities, and reduce air pollution from these facilities.

The prospective new regulations result from the findings and recommendations made by the governor's Interagency Working Group on Refinery Safety (Interagency Working Group on Refinery Safety, 2013). The governor formed the working group shortly after the August 2012 fire at the Chevron Richmond Refinery.

Under its Division of Occupational Safety and Health (Cal/OSHA), the California Department of Industrial Relations (DIR) operates a PSM unit, which enforces the state's PSM standard (Cal. Code Regs. tit. 8, § 5189) and will be charged with enforcing the new proposed PSM standard for refineries, § 5189.1.

CalEPA oversees the implementation of the CalARP program. The California Governor's Office of Emergency Services is the lead agency for the program and tracks the provisions of the PSM standard for its public health and safety and environmental implications.

Objectives

The objective of this study was to assess the overall costs and benefits of implementing the proposed changes to the PSM and CalARP regulations that govern the operation of oil and gas refineries in the state of California.

California law requires such a cost–benefit analysis, which will be conducted to meet the requirements of California Senate Bill (SB) 617 (California Department of Finance, undated). SB 617 establishes additional regulatory impact-assessment standards for major regulations. A state agency must conduct a standardized regulatory impact assessment when it estimates that a proposed regulation will have an economic impact exceeding $50 million.

In the case of the proposed regulations, refiners would likely incur additional costs for undertaking additional and enhanced PSM activities at their facilities. We examine the PSM activities that are called for in the proposed regulation. Many, if not all, of these costs will likely be passed on to California consumers in the form of higher prices for petroleum products. However, the new PSM regulations could also result in improved safety at California refineries and, in turn, result in fewer major process incidents and fewer releases of hazardous materials from refineries. Consequently, because the number of major refinery incidents (MRIs) might be reduced under the proposed regulation, the regulation could provide benefits to the public in nearby communities and might have other economic benefits, as we describe later in this report.

In this study, we conducted an assessment of the costs and the benefits of implementing the proposed regulations. We compare these costs and benefits with those in the alternative case in which the proposed regulations are not implemented.

California Oil and Gas Refineries

The proposed PSM regulation is very specific and covers only oil and gas refineries located in California. Therefore, this analysis focuses on these facilities.

The total capacity of all refineries currently operating in California is about 2 million barrels per day (bpd). The value of refined-oil and gas products that California refineries produce that is sold daily is approximately $358 million (IMPLAN 2012 data set).

In 2015, there were 12 oil and gas refineries in California. We list them in Table 1.1. Some of the refineries listed did not operate at full capacity in 2015 because of PSM incidents or because market conditions caused them to temporarily cease production of specific products.

The Phillips 66 Santa Maria Refinery is considered a part of Phillips 66's San Francisco Refinery, which is in Northern California (it is connected to it by pipeline). The capacity figure shown in Table 1.1 for Phillips 66's San Francisco Refinery includes the capacity of the Santa Maria Refinery. In addition, Paramount Petroleum groups the three refineries it owns in California (in Bakersfield, Paramount, and Long Beach) together as a single unit with a total capacity of 160,000 bpd, as shown in Table 1.1.

Figure 1.1 shows the locations of the 12 refineries listed in Table 1.1. With the exception of a few small facilities, most of the refineries in California are in or near the state's two largest cities: San Francisco and Los Angeles.

Figure 1.2 shows the Northern California refineries, five major refineries along the San Francisco Bay. Although the refineries in Northern California are across the bay from San Francisco, they are now close to multiple suburbs with significant populations. If one of these refineries were to have a major chemical accident or release (MCAR), it could affect a large number of people.

Figure 1.3 shows the Southern California refineries, seven refineries in the Los Angeles area. Several large refineries are near the Port of Long Beach in Southern California or near densely populated areas of Los Angeles in El Segundo and Torrance. If a

Table 1.1
Oil and Gas Refineries Operating in California

Refinery	Owner	Location or Locations	Capacity, in bpd
Chevron El Segundo Refinery	Chevron Corporation	El Segundo	265,000
Chevron Richmond Refinery	Chevron Corporation	Richmond	247,000
Torrance Refinery	Exxon Mobil Corporation	Torrance	155,000
Kern County Refinery	Kern Oil and Refining	Bakersfield	25,000
Paramount Petroleum Refineries	Paramount Petroleum	Paramount, Long Beach, Bakersfield	160,000
San Francisco Refinery	Phillips 66	Rodeo	110,000
Los Angeles Refinery	Phillips 66	Wilmington	135,000
Martinez Refinery	Shell Oil	Martinez	160,000
Tesoro Martinez Refinery	Tesoro Petroleum	Martinez	168,000
Los Angeles Refinery	Tesoro Petroleum	Carson	377,000
Valero Wilmington Refinery	Valero Marketing and Supply	Wilmington	80,000
Benicia Refinery	Valero Marketing and Supply	Benicia	165,000
Total capacity			2,047,000

SOURCE: California refineries' responses to our survey.

NOTE: Phillips 66 and Tesoro Petroleum operate unrelated facilities that are both formally named *Los Angeles Refinery*.

major process incident were to occur at one of the refineries in Southern California, the health of a large number of nearby residents could also be adversely affected.

Because of the hazardous chemicals that oil and gas refineries use, fatalities and serious injuries are possible not only for the workers in these facilities but also for others nearby if they are exposed to toxic chemicals that airborne plumes of smoke or particulate matter carry into nearby neighborhoods. If there were a major process incident at a refinery, significant health care costs could be incurred to respond. For example, after the Chevron Richmond Refinery fire in 2012, approximately 15,000 residents of nearby communities sought medical attention (Chevron USA Richmond Investigation Team, 2013).

Figure 1.1
California Refinery Locations

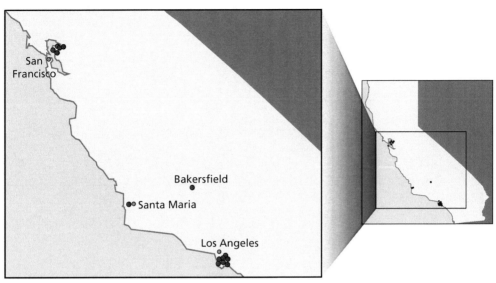

RAND *RR1421-1.1*

Figure 1.2
Refineries in Northern California

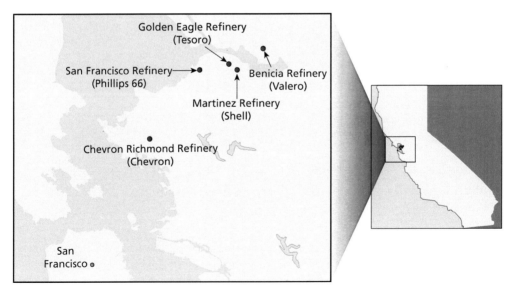

RAND *RR1421-1.2*

Figure 1.3
Refineries in Southern California

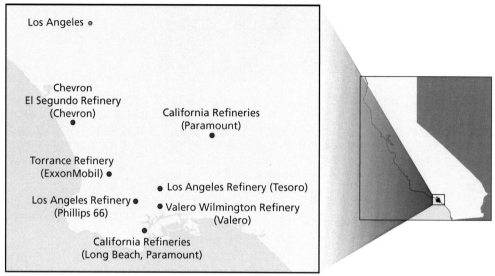

Analytical Approach

The analytical approach we used in the cost–benefit analysis considered both the costs and benefits of the proposed regulation. The analysis considered the following benefits and costs of the proposed regulation:

- costs to industry
- costs to society
- benefits to industry
- benefits to society.

Costs to industry include the implementation costs for the proposed regulation at California refineries. Refiners would pay these implementation costs, which would be a cost of doing business in the state of California. We analyze these costs across 12 major areas that the regulations cover: safety training, damage mechanism review (DMR), root-cause analysis (RCA), hierarchy-of-hazard-control analysis (HCA), process safety culture assessment (PSCA), program management (PM), performance indicators (PIs), human factors (HFs), safeguard protection analysis (SPA), layer-of-protection analysis (LOPA), process hazard analysis (PHA), and other (or undifferentiated) costs.

Costs to society include the higher cost of gasoline and jet fuel that refiners are presumed to pass through to consumers and other sectors of the California economy, such as the aviation sector. We assume that the refiners will pass the cost of implementing the proposed regulation on to California consumers in the form of higher prices for gasoline and other petroleum products.

Benefits to industry result from a potential reduction in the number of PSM MRIs at California refineries. A reduction in PSM MRIs, in turn, would result in lower workers' compensation costs, lower equipment repair costs, and increased refinery reliability and production. The first two items are costs that are avoided under the proposed regulation. The last item is an economic benefit of the proposed regulation: increased refinery output and sales.

Additional qualitative benefits to society could result from the implementation of the proposed regulations. These include the potential reduction in worker fatalities, fatalities of nearby community members, and a potential reduction in worker and community-member injuries. These potential benefits would also translate in cost savings, including lower health care costs for residents of nearby communities, and lower local government costs, including costs for first responders' overtime during refinery process incidents. We examine each of these costs and benefits in detail later in this report.

Estimating Regulation Implementation Costs

For this analysis, we used cost and safety information that each of the 12 refineries in California provided. We gathered this information during the course of structured interviews with refinery personnel and in written responses. During these discussions, we also elicited refiners' opinions on the changes in safety procedures and management practices that would be required under the proposed refinery PSM regulations. Each of these changes will have cost implications.

To ensure the independence of the research team and to promote an open and frank dialogue with refinery operators, regulators were not present during these meetings. In addition, we signed nondisclosure agreements (NDAs) with each of the 12 refiners. The refiners have designated the written responses and specific cost figures that the refiners provided during the information-gathering sessions as proprietary information protected under the terms of the NDAs. Consequently, we do not include the cost estimates of individual refiners in this report. To prevent the disclosure of proprietary information, we report only the range of cost estimates that the refiners provided, along with other statistical measures, as described in Chapters Three and Four.

By eliciting cost information from refiners, we ensured that estimates were coming from sources with direct knowledge of refinery costs. Although we took steps to minimize the presence of regulator bias by conducting these interviews under NDAs, the approach invites speculation about the presence of industry bias that might lead to inflated estimates in an effort to avoid future regulation. We sought to minimize this effect by asking detailed questions about specific parts of the regulation and then cross-checking the results from one refiner to the next. Although there was significant variance in the results, these seemed to reflect legitimate differences of opinion about how the regulations would be implemented and how much compliance might cost. We discussed the few outlying estimates with the refiners and either revised them upon further clarification of the questions or retained them as legitimately different estimates. In general, however, the estimates for each part of the regulation were consistent from one refiner to another. This consistency, in the apparent absence of coordination, gives us some confidence in the accuracy, or at least honesty, of the estimates. To the extent that this approach has biased the estimates, we would expect it to lead to an overstatement of costs—making the proposed regulations look less cost-effective than they might actually be.

Macroeconomic Analysis

A major part of the analysis is to estimate the macroeconomic impact that the proposed regulations could have on the economy of California. These fall into two broad categories: the labor employment benefits of implementing the proposed regulation in the California refinery sector and the impact on California consumers. For the latter, we include the macroeconomic impact on California consumers in terms of the price of gasoline.

These costs and benefits will accrue over time and will affect the California economy over time. We have mapped these costs to inputs to IMPLAN, a leading and widely used input–output economic analysis tool for assessing the regional macroeconomic impacts of policy decisions.[1] We used the IMPLAN model results to identify the proposed regulations' impacts on the economy of the state of California.

We consider the costs that California consumers would avoid if the number of MRIs were reduced under the proposed regulations. If a major incident were to occur at a California refinery, gasoline production at that facility could be halted, and the price of gasoline in the state could rise. This is a cost that California consumers would pay and would be the cost that they could avoid under the proposed regulations. We used the IMPLAN model to assess the macroeconomic impact that MRIs and outages could have on the economy of California—in particular, on the California gross state product (GSP).

We also enumerate nonmonetary benefits of the proposed regulation, including those for public health, safety, welfare, and environment, by estimating the costs avoided when MRIs are avoided.

Classifying Process Safety Management Major Refinery Incidents and Estimating Their Likelihood

PSM MRIs are rare events in California and the United States, but, when they do occur, they can have a major economic impact, result in worker deaths and injuries,

---

[1] Information about the IMPLAN model is available at IMPLAN Group, undated.

and lead to major adverse health consequences for those in nearby communities. Each refinery is required to provide federal, state, and local government officials with a risk management plan (RMP) that includes a description of the worst-case refinery-incident scenarios based on the types and amounts of hazardous chemicals present at the facility. We reviewed California refinery RMPs and the worst-case scenarios for most of the refineries. We use RMP worst-case scenarios and historical data on MRIs in California to estimate the likelihood, size, and impact of possible future MRIs.

We also investigate process MRI rates under different regulatory environments and describe how one can use these data to estimate the likelihood of these incidents under the proposed and current regulations and the costs that could be avoided under the proposed regulation. As part of this analysis, we examine worker fatalities under different regulatory environments and estimate the likelihood that worker fatalities will decrease and by how much under the proposed regulation. We also examine the even smaller subset of MRIs that prove especially costly to the California economy. The latter type of incident is important because, although these events occur even less frequently than other incidents, they have an outsize macroeconomic impact on the state economy. Finally, we examine the statistical significance of all these results.

Break-Even Analysis

We compare the costs and benefits of the proposed regulation using a break-even approach. In this approach, we compare the costs of implementing the regulation and the potential cost savings that could be incurred by having fewer MRIs in California.

This quantitative break-even analysis incorporates costs and benefits that can be quantified with authoritative data sources. We present details of this approach in Chapter Three.

Organization of This Report

We organize the remainder of this report as follows. In Chapter Two, we provide an overview of the proposed regulations and describe the motivation for their creation. We also highlight the differences between the proposed regulation and current PSM regulations. Chapter Three provides a detailed discussion of the methodology used in this cost–benefit analysis. Included in this discussion are the structured interview questions that we used to gather information from each of the refiners and a description of the macroeconomic models used in the analysis. Chapter Four provides a detailed description of the estimated costs for implementing the proposed regulations. Chapter Five includes a historical analysis of California refinery process incidents, including those that have occurred within Contra Costa County under the Contra Costa County industrial safety ordinance (ISO), and other incidents that have occurred elsewhere in the state under current California PSM regulations. Chapter Six provides a review of

California and U.S. gasoline price trends of the past several decades. The chapter also describes a California gas price model that can be used to assess the impact that MRIs can have on California gas prices. Chapter Seven includes the macroeconomic impact analysis for the proposed regulation. Chapter Eight examines the potential benefits of the proposed regulation and the costs that refiners could avoid if the number of MRIs is reduced. Chapter Nine looks at the balance of costs and benefits of implementing the proposed regulation and includes a break-even analysis of same. The report ends with Chapter Ten, which relates the study's conclusions.

CHAPTER TWO

Overview of the Proposed Regulations

Motivation for the Proposed Refinery Regulations

A major fire at the Chevron refinery in Richmond in August 2012 raised public concern about refinery safety in California. A hydrocarbon vapor cloud engulfed 19 employees who narrowly escaped serious injury and death (see Figure 2.1). The fire created a large smoke plume that spread far beyond the refinery, causing a reported 15,000 people to seek medical attention.

Several agencies investigated the incident, including Cal/OSHA, the U.S. Chemical Safety and Hazard Investigation Board (CSB), and the U.S. Environmental Protection Agency. The CSB issued several investigative reports about this incident, the first being an interim investigation report that described the corrosion processes that led to the pipe failure that caused the fire (CSB, 2013). All these investigations found significant safety-system problems and PSM deficiencies that led to the incident (CSB, 2014, 2015).

Basis for New Refinery Regulations

The Governor's Working Group

In October 2012, Governor Jerry Brown formed the Interagency Working Group on Refinery Safety to identify ways of improving refinery and state-agency performance. These agencies met for eight months and identified regulatory gaps. Although refineries in California are subject to regulation by many agencies, the working group determined that additional measures, including new approaches, would enhance prevention and risk reduction.

The working-group examination included how to prevent refinery incidents that threaten workers, communities, and the environment and how to promote a culture of safety and prevention of hazards.

The final report of the governor's Interagency Working Group on Refinery Safety, *Improving Public and Worker Safety at Oil Refineries*, published in February 2014, rec-

Figure 2.1
Chevron Richmond Refinery Incident, August 13, 2012

SOURCE: CSB, 2015, p. i.
RAND *RR1421-2.1*

ommended contemplated changes to the PSM and CalARP regulations (Interagency Working Group on Refinery Safety, 2013).

Interagency Refinery Working Group drafted amendments to the CalARP program and the PSM regulation, proposed by Cal/OSHA, part of DIR. The content of both regulations is very similar. The PSM regulation focuses on minimizing risks to employees, whereas the CalARP regulation focuses on protecting the safety and health of the community, as well as the environment.

Actions Already Taken on Refinery Safety

After the Chevron Richmond fire, the California State Legislature approved a budget that added new inspector positions to the Cal/OSHA PSM unit. These positions are funded through Cal/OSHA's fee authority.

On August 5, 2013, the California attorney general and the district attorney for Contra Costa County filed a criminal action against Chevron in response to the August 6, 2012, incident. Pursuant to a plea agreement, Chevron agreed to pay $2 million in fines and restitution and pleaded no contest to six misdemeanor counts; the company was placed on three and a half years of probation at the Richmond refinery. The settlement included such requirements as abatement of problems identified in Cal/OSHA's review of certain piping inspections and revised procedures for Chevron's DMRs.

Brown signed SB 54 into law on October 13, 2013. The legislation requires that certain facilities, including refineries, use contractors that employ a trained workforce in the building and construction trades. This legislation seeks to address concerns that some stakeholders raised about the adequacy of the training of contract workers.

Changes and Differences Between Current and Proposed Regulations

The PSM and CalARP revisions consist of nine new subsections and revisions to the remaining 15 subsections. After consultation with both regulators and refiners, we grouped the regulatory changes into 12 categories: safety training, DMR, RCA, HCA, PSCA, PM, PIs, HFs, SPA, LOPA, PHA, and other (or undifferentiated) costs. Many provisions of the proposed regulation have generated controversy within the oil and gas industry. Discussions with government officials and refinery operators revealed significantly different interpretations of key provisions of the draft regulation.

The legislature gave the refiners and us a draft version of the proposed regulation to support the cost-estimation process in May 2015 (Cal/OSHA, 2015). This draft is now available to the general public for review at the same online location (Cal/OSHA, 2015). The rest of this section provides excerpts from this May 15, 2015, working version of the PSM regulation that the refinery operators used to develop their implementation cost estimates. These excerpts describe six key new requirements. Several of these new requirements raised cost-of-implementation concerns among refiners and could be interpreted in different ways with different cost implications. We highlight these sections in bold.

Hierarchy-of-Hazard-Control Analysis and Inherently Safer Measures
HCA is

> [a] procedure that applies the Hierarchy of Hazard Controls for the purpose of selecting recommendations that eliminate or minimize a hazard, or that reduce the risk presented by a hazard. (Cal/OSHA, 2015, p. 4)

Inherent safety

> focuses on eliminating or reducing . . . hazards. . . . A process is inherently safer if it reduces or eliminates the hazards associated with materials or operations used in the process, and this reduction or elimination is permanent and inseparable from the material or operation. A process with reduced hazards is described as inher-

ently safer compared to a process with only passive, active, and procedural safeguards. (Cal/OSHA, 2015, p. 4)

The HCA

> shall . . . identify and evaluate all relevant inherent safety measures and safeguards (or where appropriate, combinations of measures and safeguards) in an iterative manner to reduce each risk to the greatest extent feasible. These inherent safety measures and safeguards shall include the following: 1. All control techniques or management systems that have been achieved in practice for the petroleum refining and related industrial sectors; and, 2. Control techniques or management systems that have been required or recommended for the petroleum refining industry and, where applicable, related industrial sectors in a regulation or report by a federal, state or local agency. (Cal/OSHA, 2015, pp. 19–20)

> In conducting the HCA, the team shall select and recommend first and second order inherent safety measures unless the team can demonstrate in writing it is not feasible to do so. Where the team does not recommend a first or second order inherent safety measure, the team shall document and justify in writing: (A) why that inherent safety measure is not feasible; and (B) why the inherent safety measure(s) and/or safeguards the team has recommended are the most protective feasible alternative. (Cal/OSHA, 2015, p. 20)

Process Safety Culture Assessment
Process safety culture is

> [t]he core values and behaviors resulting from a collective commitment by leaders and individuals that emphasize process safety over competing goals in order to ensure protection of people and the environment. (Cal/OSHA, 2015, p. 6)

> The employer shall develop, implement and maintain an effective Process Safety Culture Assessment (PSCA) program. . . . The . . . PSCA shall . . . evaluate process safety culture practices and, at a minimum, assess progress with regard to the following: (A) Encouragement for reporting of process safety concerns; (B) Ensuring that reward or incentive programs do not deter reporting by employees of process safety concerns, near misses, injuries and incidents; (C) Ensuring that process safety is not compromised by production pressures; and, (D) Promoting effective process safety leadership at all levels of the organization. (Cal/OSHA, 2015, p. 25)

Damage Mechanism Reviews

The employer shall complete a Damage Mechanism Review (DMR) within five (5) years of the effective date of this Section for each process for which a damage mechanism exists. . . . The DMR shall be performed by a team with expertise in engineering, operation of the process or processes under review, equipment and pipe inspection, and damage and failure mechanisms. The team shall include one member knowledgeable in the specific DMR methodology being used. The employer shall provide for employee participation in this process, pursuant to subsection (q). (Cal/OSHA, 2015, p. 17)

DMRs shall include an assessment of previous experience with the process, including the inspection history and all damage mechanism data; a review of industry-wide experience with the process; and applicable standards, codes and practices. (Cal/OSHA, 2015, p. 18)

Human Factors

The human factors program shall evaluate staffing levels; the complexity of tasks; the length of time needed to complete tasks; the level of training, experience and expertise of employees; the human–machine and human–system interface; the physical challenges of the work environment in which the task is performed; employee fatigue and other effects of shiftwork and overtime; communication systems; and the understandability and clarity of operating and maintenance procedures. (Cal/OSHA, 2015, p. 26)

The employer shall include an analysis of human factors in the design phase of major changes and in all incident investigations, PHAs, MOOCs [managements of organizational change], and HCAs. (Cal/OSHA, 2015, p. 27)

Safeguard Protection Analysis

For each process, the employer shall perform a written Safeguard Protection Analysis (SPA) where a PHA identifies the potential for a major incident, to determine (A) the effectiveness of existing individual safeguards; (B) the combined effectiveness of all existing safeguards for each failure scenario in the PHA; (C) the individual and combined effectiveness of safeguards recommended in the PHA; and (D) the individual and combined effectiveness of additional or alternative safeguards that may be needed. (Cal/OSHA, 2015, p. 28)

All safeguards for each failure scenario shall be independent of each other and independent of initiating causes. (Cal/OSHA, 2015, p. 28)

The SPA shall utilize a quantitative or semi-quantitative method, such as Layer of Protection Analysis (LOPA) or an equally effective method. The SPA may be a stand-alone analysis or may be incorporated into the PHA. (Cal/OSHA, 2015, p. 28)

The SPA shall include a written report of findings, conclusions and recommendations, including additional or alternative safeguards that will reduce the risk of a major incident. **The team shall select and recommend the most protective safeguards, unless the team can demonstrate in writing that it is not feasible to do so. Where the team does not recommend the most protective safeguards, the team shall document and justify in writing (A) why the safeguard is not feasible; and (B) why the safeguards the team has recommended are the most protective feasible alternative.** (Cal/OSHA, 2015, p. 29)

The employer shall implement all recommendations, pursuant to subsection (y). (Cal/OSHA, 2015, p. 29)

Section (y), Implementation, addresses the recommendations as follows:

The employer may change or reject a team recommendation if the employer can demonstrate that the recommendation meets one of the following conditions: (A) The analysis upon which the recommendation is based contains material factual errors; (B) The recommendation is not relevant to process safety; (C) An alternative measure would provide an equivalent or better level of protection . . . ; or, (D) The recommendation is infeasible. (Cal/OSHA, 2015, p. 32)

The draft defines *feasible* as

[c]apable of being accomplished in a successful manner within a reasonable period of time, taking into account health, safety, economic, environmental, legal, social and technological factors. (Cal/OSHA, 2015, p. 3)

It should be noted that the definition of *feasible* in the regulation has been a concern of refiners because it could imply that refiners will be forced to make very expensive repairs in response to SPA and LOPA recommendations (see bold text above). However, the *feasible* definition provided in the proposed regulation does explicitly state that economic factors can be taken into account in determining what a feasible process system design or repair is.

Recognized and Generally Accepted Good Engineering Practices
The draft regulation defines *recognized and generally accepted good engineering practices* (RAGAGEP) as follows:

Engineering, operation, or maintenance activities established in codes, standards, technical reports or recommended practices and published by the American Institute of Chemical Engineers (AIChE), American National Standards Institute (ANSI), American Petroleum Institute (API), American Society of Heating, Refrigeration, and Air Conditioning Engineers (ASHRAE), American Society of Mechanical Engineers (ASME), American Society of Testing and Materials

(ASTM), Center for Chemical Process Safety (CCPS), National Fire Protection Association (NFPA), and Instrument Society of America (ISA), or other standard setting organizations. **RAGAGEP does not include standards, guidelines or practices developed for internal use by the employer.** (Cal/OSHA, 2015, p. 6)

The mechanical-integrity (MI) element includes these RAGAGEP requirements:

Inspections and tests shall be performed on process equipment, using procedures that meet or exceed RAGAGEP. (Cal/OSHA, 2015, p. 16)

The frequency of inspections and tests shall be consistent with the applicable manufacturer's recommendations or RAGAGEP, whichever is more frequent. Inspections and tests shall be conducted more frequently if necessary, based on the operating experience with the process equipment. (Cal/OSHA, 2015, p. 16)

The employer shall correct deficiencies in process equipment consistent with RAGAGEP or other equally protective standards that ensure safe operation. (Cal/OSHA, 2015, p. 16)

If the employer installs new process equipment or has existing equipment for which no RAGAGEP exists, the employer shall ensure that this equipment is designed, constructed, installed, maintained, inspected, tested and operated in a safe manner. (Cal/OSHA, 2015, p. 16)

The process safety information element requires the following:

The employer shall document that process equipment complies with RAGAGEP, where RAGAGEP has been established for that process equipment, or with other equally protective standards that ensure safe operation. If the employer installs new process equipment for which no RAGAGEP exists, the employer shall document that this equipment is designed, constructed, installed, maintained, inspected, tested and operated in a safe manner. (Cal/OSHA, 2015, p. 8)

Additional new or significantly changed elements in the proposed PSM regulation (Cal/OSHA, 2015) include

- incident investigation and RCA
- MOOC
- PSM management system
- access to documents and information
- implementation
- HCA method.

Summary of Significant New Requirements

The proposed PSM standard contains 24 elements (sections). Nine of these elements are new. There are revisions to the 15 existing elements, but significant changes are primarily in the new elements briefly summarized below. Also included is a summary of a major new requirement in the existing PHA element, which requires that a SPA be performed. We provide the full text of the proposed regulation in the appendix of this report.

Damage Mechanism Review

Each refiner should perform a DMR for each process for which a damage mechanism exists. This includes examination of mechanical loading, erosion, corrosion, thermal-related failures, cracking, and embrittlement. A DMR must include an assessment of previous experience with the process, including the inspection history, as well as a review of industry-wide experience and applicable standards, codes, and practices.

Hierarchy-of-Hazard-Control Analysis

Each refiner should conduct an HCA as a stand-alone analysis for all processes. It should identify inherent safety measures from most preferred to least preferred. These include first- and second-order inherent-safety measures, as well as passive, active, and procedural safeguards. It should eliminate hazards to the greatest extent feasible using first-order inherent-safety measures.

Safeguard Protection Analysis, Part of the Process Hazard Analysis Element

Each refiner should perform a SPA to determine the effectiveness of individual and combined safeguards. Safeguards must be independent of each other. The SPA must examine the likelihood and severity of potential initiating events, including equipment failures, human errors, loss of flow, pressure, temperature, and level control. It must also evaluate excess reaction and external events.

Process Safety Culture Assessment

Each refiner should implement a PSCA program that includes evaluation of the hazard reporting program and response to reports of hazards. Also it should perform an evaluation to ensure that incentive programs do not discourage reporting of hazards and that process safety is prioritized during upset or emergency conditions.

Human Factors

Each refiner should establish a human-factor program that includes analysis of human factors in the design phase of major changes and in incident investigations, PHAs, MOOCs, and HCAs. It should evaluate staffing levels, complexity, and time needed to do tasks, as well as employees' levels of training, experience, and expertise. Evaluations must also include the human–machine interface, physical challenges in the work environment, employee fatigue, and the effects of shiftwork and overtime, as well as the clarity of operating and maintenance procedures.

Management of Organizational Change

Each refiner should conduct a MOOC assessment prior to reducing staffing or changing experience levels, making alterations in shift duration, or increasing employee responsibilities. It should perform a MOOC for changes affecting operations, engineering, maintenance, health and safety, and emergency response. Also included is an evaluation of the use of contractors in permanent positions. Each MOOC must include an analysis of human factors.

Compliance Audits

Each refiner should conduct a compliance audit every three years and issue a written report of the findings, including all deficiencies identified. The audit must include recommendations and corrective actions taken. The report must identify the qualifications of the people performing the audit. The audit team must consult with operators who have expertise and experience in each process.

Process Safety Management Program

Each refiner should implement a PSM program, which is updated at least every three years and includes an organizational chart that identifies personnel responsible for implementing the PSM program. Process safety performance indicators must be tracked and documented.

Division Access to Documents and Information

Each refiner should provide all documents and information developed or collected pursuant to the PSM regulation to Cal/OSHA upon request.

Implementation

Each refiner should establish a corrective action program to prioritize the recommendations of a PHA, SPA, DMR, HCA, incident investigation, PSCA, human-factor analysis, or compliance audit. Any recommendation that meets one of the following criteria could be rejected: (1) The analysis on which the recommendation is based contains material factual errors; (2) the recommendation is not relevant to process safety; or (3) the recommendation is infeasible (however, a determination of infeasibility cannot be based solely on cost).

CHAPTER THREE

Methodology

The proposed refinery regulations are intended to prevent low-probability, high-consequence events that can cause serious damage to facilities and property near refineries and that can seriously harm the health and welfare of people living in nearby communities. In addition, such events could also adversely affect other nearby industries and cause secondary economic impacts. Because of the complexity of this analytical problem of deriving costs and benefits of the proposed regulation, we chose to use different complementary methods to estimate these costs and benefits. As discussed in this chapter, a wide range of cost effects is possible. Therefore, it is important for us to consider which costs would have the greatest impact on the California economy and on the largest number of California residents.

Costs and Benefits Considered

In its request for proposals (RFP), the state of California laid out a broad set of costs and benefits to be considered. The following list, based on the RFP, outlines the costs and benefits that we considered in this study:

- costs to industry
  - conducting analyses required in the regulatory revisions
  - correcting deferred maintenance and making repairs that the new regulatory requirements make necessary (that is, beyond those that would be scheduled as part of normal maintenance in the absence of the new regulatory requirements)
  - implementing management and programmatic changes to improve safety
  - implementing inherently safer systems and additional safeguards in some cases
- costs to society
  - pass-through of certain industry costs, including higher price of gasoline to California consumers
  - other
- benefits to industry: costs avoided
  - MRIs (including catastrophic events and upset events)

- civil penalties
- benefits to industry: safety improvements
  - costs avoided—value of lost refinery production and sales
- benefits to society: costs avoided
  - costs to consumers of increased gasoline prices
  - health care costs
  - emergency services
  - medical claims
- benefits to society: improvements
  - fewer refinery-worker deaths
  - changes in employment
  - uninterrupted fuel supply
  - uninterrupted employment in the oil sector.

We could not estimate some costs because of a lack of data. These include criminal liability charges, reputation damage, infrastructure impacts, air-quality damage, and property-value damage.

As the list indicates, this report explicitly addresses costs and benefits to industry and society in many dimensions. We gave more attention to the cost and benefit categories that have the greatest impact on the California economy because these factors will likely drive the analysis of the utility of the proposed regulations. Framed in these terms, the costs and benefits not quantified in this analysis are likely to be relatively small. We considered all costs and benefits in a macroeconomic context in order both to understand their impact on the broader California economy and to avoid double-counting of pass-through costs and related costs and benefits that might potentially be counted in more than one category.

Cost to Industry and Society Estimates

We treat costs to industry in considerable quantitative detail using structured interview techniques (described below) to elicit best estimates from the refiners themselves. We incorporated all subheadings of cost into the interview questions and produced meaningful estimates. Although the industry-expert elicitation has the potential to produce inflated cost estimates because of industry bias, we use an approach designed to minimize these effects as described in the "Analytical Approach" section of Chapter One. We found other approaches to estimating the cost of the proposed regulations—including comparison to historical precedents and direct modeling of costs—to be unworkable because of a lack of data and specialized knowledge of refinery operations that we would require to make high-quality estimates. We also consider costs to society quantitatively, in a macroeconomic context, to be primarily pass-through of industry costs.

Given the survey responses, we calculated the additional costs that industry would incur to comply with the proposed regulations. We calculated costs in 12 major areas that the regulations cover: safety training, DMR, RCA, HCA, PSCA, PM, PIs, HFs, SPA, LOPA, PHA, and other (or undifferentiated) costs. We essentially took refiners' estimates at face value as good-faith estimates of cost coming from those in the best position to understand refinery costs.

Benefits to Industry

Refiners were less able to identify benefits of the regulations or share this type of information with us. Refiners were reluctant to share facility repair costs that MRIs caused. They were also reluctant to share the amount of production output lost as a result of past incidents because this and related information is considered highly proprietary in the refinery industry. Despite this, we believe that it is possible to estimate the amount of revenue lost in at least some types of refinery incidents, as we describe later in this report. Refiners were similarly unable to identify benefits of improved refinery operations stemming from the regulations (for example, improved system reliability). We avoided speculating about the possible benefits of such operational improvements because no solid data were available on which to base objective estimates of savings brought about by such factors as improved reliability.

We did estimate the proposed regulation's benefits to industry by estimating the revenue loss that would be avoided if the proposed regulation is implemented and by estimating how the probability of a major incident would decrease as a result of proposed regulations.

Benefits to Society

Similarly, we estimated benefits to society from costs avoided based on examining historical incidents and considering the expected savings from reduced probability of future MRIs.

We did this by estimating the past incidents' costs to the California economy and examining how the probability of such events could be reduced in the future as a result of the proposed regulation.

Costs of MRIs that we tallied include the cost of emergency services and estimated medical claims by injured workers and residents. We also acknowledge damage to air quality and property values but have not valued them in dollar terms in this report. Also included in this analysis is the increase in gas prices that would likely occur as a result of an MRI.

In Chapter Six, we also consider other improvements to the California economy that result from implementing the proposed regulations, such as increased employment.

Interview Process

We used a structured interview survey instrument to collect cost and benefit data directly from California refiners. Because the set of questions was extensive and the proposed regulatory environment is not yet well defined or understood, we met with each refiner for one to two hours to discuss the questions. We made every effort to ensure that the refiners answered the questions from a consistent understanding of their scope, meaning, and intent. In the course of these interviews, we did not attempt to interpret or clarify the proposed regulations. We aimed all discussion of the nature of the regulations at giving us a clear understanding of how each refiner interprets the evolving rules.

Structured Interview Questions

We used the detailed set of questions in an effort to glean consistent information in an extremely uncertain environment. We reproduce these questions in the appendix. The questions attempt to break costs down in a systematic way that will be recognizable to refinery PSM experts. They further attempt to elicit enough context for the answers to allow us to identify which costs are marginal costs that the regulations add (these are the focus of this study) and which are total or historical safety-related costs. They further attempt to elicit a sense of timing: what costs are initial start-up costs and which are long-term annual costs.

We initially based these questions on a cost worksheet that DIR developed, then enhanced and extended them based on our understanding of the regulatory and refinery environment, and further adjusted them in response to questions and suggestions generated during meetings with refiners.

We asked refiners to submit written answers to the interview questions approximately two weeks after the orientation meeting. Although this compressed time frame was challenging for refiners, they generally produced well-reasoned responses that were, for the most part, both internally consistent and reasonably consistent from one refiner to the next. There was some unevenness in response quality, with a few refiners providing aggregated numbers, or numbers for major categories only, without further explanation or detail. The vast majority of refiners, however, answered all subquestions in some detail. This provided us with sufficient context to make sense of the less contextualized responses.

Macroeconomic Modeling

In order to assess the proposed regulations' secondary, macroeconomic impacts on the state of California, we used the IMPLAN social accounting matrix model. IMPLAN is an input–output model of the U.S. economy that is widely used to assess regional economic impacts.

Input–output models, such as IMPLAN, are designed to understand the interactions between sectors of an economy. IMPLAN, as it is currently implemented, is based on the methods that Wassily Leontief developed and documented in *The Structure of the American Economy, 1919–1929: An Empirical Application of Equilibrium Analysis* (Leontief, 1941) and *Studies in the Structure of the American Economy: Theoretical and Empirical Explorations in Input–Output Analysis* (Leontief, 1953). This method for modeling the flow of shocks, both positive and negative, through the economy was recognized with the Sveriges Riksbank Prize in Economic Sciences in Memory of Alfred Nobel in 1973. An input–output model is a representation of the linkages between major sectors of a regional economy and, to a lesser extent, the linkages to the rest of the country and the rest of the world. Each sector is assumed to require inputs from other sectors in order to produce output. These inputs come both from the regional economy under consideration and from foreign and domestic imports. The model traces the path of production in order to satisfy final demand across industries and sectors taking into account that a dollar of demand in one sector will stimulate demands for inputs across other regional sectors, generating additional demand.

Industry and academia use IMPLAN widely. In recent studies, the oil and gas industry has used IMPLAN for macroeconomic studies in California (Western States Petroleum Association, undated).

IMPLAN provides data on an annual basis for all inputs to production, outputs from production, and the distribution of final consumption across households and various levels of government at the county level for 440 distinct industry sectors. These county-level data can then be aggregated to form an economy of a region, state, or the entire nation. One of the major assumptions that underlie the input–output modeling framework is that production takes place with Leontief production functions. Leontief production functions assume that production takes place with fixed ratios of specific inputs, implying that there is no substitution across inputs. This modeling framework allows for a relatively simple analysis of the economic impact for a wide variety of policy and business shocks to the economy. Because of the linkages across the economy, one sector's \$1 increase in output can have more than a \$1 impact on the economy. This is the notion commonly referred to as the multiplier effect that underlies much of the discussion of economic impacts. The IMPLAN model allows an analyst a relatively easy means of implementing such analyses in both single-region and multiregion models.

There are three main drawbacks to the input–output modeling framework. First, the Leontief production function does not allow any substitution across inputs to production. If the price of an input rises, input costs simply rise because of the fixed ratios of inputs that the Leontief production function assumes. Second, there are no prices—only total values. Taken together, analysis of tax policy, which alters relative prices, or substitution across inputs causes a problem for input–output models. Finally, the base-year (2012) data are used to project into the future. This assumes that the production "recipe" stays fixed over the long term and that there are no increases in technology. Hence, the further out a projection is made, the greater the error because of the inflexibility of the production function.

An alternative to the input–output model is a calibrated, computable general equilibrium (CGE) model. CGEs relax the assumption of Leontief production and usually assume either a constant elasticity of substitution or nested constant-elasticity-of-substitution production function. This allows for greater flexibility regarding the substitution pattern across inputs. Additionally, prices are allowed to adjust to policy or economic shocks to the economy. CGEs for regional economies of the United States are usually calibrated using the IMPLAN data because the model assumes that the IMPLAN data are in equilibrium. One of the main advantages of using a CGE framework as opposed to an input–output framework is the ability to assess a wider set of economic impacts.

Because our preliminary cost and economic analysis indicated relatively small changes in the price of refinery output (primarily gasoline), we determined that IMPLAN's simplicity and transparency made it a suitable tool for assessing economic impacts in this case. To the extent that the use of an input–output model introduces biases as compared with a full CGE model (e.g., Regional Economic Models, Inc.), that bias would be toward showing slightly larger economic impacts. Because an input–output model does not allow for substitution based on relative prices, it tends to capture maximum effects. For example, a significantly higher cost of gasoline might lead to greater adoption of electric cars, leading to lower demand for gasoline and thus a secondary reduction in the cost of gasoline. Whereas a CGE model can represent this secondary adaptive effect, the input–output model cannot. However, given the modest price impacts indicated by the cost data collected, we estimate that these effects will be small and well within the general margin of error for the study overall.

Costs of Major Refinery Incidents

Every refinery incident is unique, and serious incidents are relatively rare. MRIs are low-probability events. This makes precise estimation of the cost of a typical incident difficult: There are so few cases to consider.

In this report, we review several definitions of *MRI* and the history of such incidents at California refineries. We find that some MRIs have little or no economic consequence, while others (an small subset of an already small set) are high-consequence events. We call the latter high-consequence MRIs costly MRIs (CMRIs). We show that they cause high costs for refiners and even higher costs for the public. In addition, they can cause the death and serious injury of workers at the facility and serious adverse health effects to nearby residents. In the worst-case scenarios, in which a large quantity of hazardous materials at the refinery is released into the community, a significant number of nearby residents could die. Fortunately, to date, an incident of this magnitude has not occurred in California or the United States.

In this study, we did not speculate on the costs, deaths, or injuries that could result from hypothetical worst possible refinery incidents. Instead, we use historical data on actual refinery incidents that have taken place in California to estimate these costs.

We use historical data from three well-documented CMRIs that occurred in California in the past 16 years (a time period for which we have data of reasonable quality). We developed an estimate of these costs by examining the 1999 Tosco incident, the 2012 Chevron Richmond incident, and the 2015 ExxonMobil Torrance incident. For the Richmond case, we obtained data on local government response costs directly from Contra Costa County. Chevron also provided an accounting of incident-related costs that it reimbursed to various governments and community members to cover emergency response, health, and postincident recovery and planning activities.

Neither ExxonMobil nor Chevron refiners were willing to divulge estimates of the cost of repairs or of downtime resulting from these incidents. However, we were able to obtain an estimate of the repair costs for the 1999 Tosco refinery incident from a publicly available press report (Tansey, 2000). We use this in our calculations.

We note that the increase in the price of gasoline resulting from supply shortages that these incidents created could partially offset any lost revenues for a refiner that suffers an outage and a production loss but that operates more than one refinery in the state. This impact can complicate making a net calculation of the economic impact of the incidents on the refiners themselves.

Despite this complication, we determined that refinery-repair costs and refinery production losses for an MRI were relatively small given the macroeconomic costs on the California economy that the increased price of gasoline causes. For this reason, we focus much of our macroeconomic analysis on the latter costs. We do, however, discuss costs to industry of MRIs.

Break-Even Analysis Approach

To compare costs and benefits of the proposed regulation, we use a break-even approach, in which we compare the costs of implementing the regulation and the potential cost savings that could be incurred under the new regulation by reducing the number of CMRIs and the consequences of such incidents.

We estimate the incremental benefit of the proposed regulation as the reduction in the risk of a CMRI brought about the regulation (i.e., a risk reduction). Risk, R, is often equated with the probability, P, that an event will occur (in this case, a CMRI) multiplied by the consequence, C, of the event (in this case, that the incident will have a major economic impact on the state of California): $R = P \times C$.

The incremental reduction in risk from the proposed regulation can be expressed as $\Delta R = R_p - R_c = P_p C_p - P_c C_c$, where the subscript c refers to conditions under the current regulation and the subscript p refers to conditions under the proposed regulation.

In this report, we examine the probability of refinery incidents and the number of refinery incidents under different regulatory regimes in the state of California. We find evidence to support the assertion that P_p is lower than P_c.

However, we do not find evidence that the consequences of MRIs will be reduced under the proposed regulations, i.e., that $C_c - C_p > 0$. The costly major incidents that have occurred have varied significantly in consequence (they have high variance). Furthermore, understanding the mechanisms by which the proposed regulation could reduce consequence requires detailed engineering analysis of refinery process management systems, which is beyond the scope of this investigation.

Consequently, we assume that $C_p = C_c = C$ and approximate the risk reduction as $\Delta R = (P_p - P_c)C = \Delta P \times C$.

It should be noted that this is a conservative assumption that might underestimate the benefit of the proposed regulation.

Because risk is the product of probability of events occurring and consequences of those events, it can be presented in terms of an annual expected loss, E. We then use an approach adapted from one used in terrorism risk analysis (Willis and LaTourrette, 2008) to set the critical risk-reduction factor to be

$$Cr = \frac{\Delta R}{R_c} = \frac{E_c - E_p}{E_c}.$$

In Chapter Nine, we describe the details of this analysis.

CHAPTER FOUR

Implementation Costs of the Proposed Regulation

Refinery Regulation Implementation Costs

We estimated the total implementation cost for all of the refineries in California by aggregating estimates from the structured interview surveys described above and reproduced in the appendix. The quality of data reported for one-time, up-front costs was much lower than that reported for ongoing costs. The majority of refiners indicated up-front costs that were relatively minor given the ongoing costs—in the area of 20 percent to 80 percent of a single year's cost. One refiner reported anticipating extremely significant start-up costs in a single PSM category; we discuss this estimate separately. Because ongoing costs made up the bulk of the reported costs and were more consistently reported by refiners, the following section focuses on these ongoing costs.

Types of Costs Considered for Implementation of the Proposed Regulations

Given the survey responses, we calculated the additional costs that industry would incur to comply with the proposed regulations. We calculated costs in 12 major areas that the regulations cover: safety training, DMR, RCA, HCA, PSCA, PM, PIs, HFs, SPA, LOPA, PHA, and other (or undifferentiated) costs. We essentially took refiners' estimates at face value as good-faith estimates of cost coming from those in the best position to understand refinery costs.

We took care to aggregate only costs stemming from the new regulations. In some cases, refiners reported the total cost of programs that are already in place and that the new regulations might make more expensive. In these cases, we included in the aggregate expense only the additional expense. Similarly, when tabulating the proposed regulations' costs, we excluded any safety-related initiatives already under way that the regulations do not directly mandate.

Methods Used to Obtain Average, High, and Low Cost Estimates

We used variation between these estimates as the basis for estimating the range of actual costs—assuming that some refiners might miss the mark on either the low or high end. To produce the range of possible costs, we first normalized each refiner's cost by the refinery's capacity as measured in barrels per day. We explored various approaches to normalizing unit costs, including cost per refinery (unnormalized), cost per barrel per day of capacity, and cost per PSM process. We found none of these normalization approaches to be entirely satisfactory but determined that normalization by capacity produced the greatest reduction in the variance of estimates and captured the broad idea of larger refineries being more expensive to operate than smaller ones. We then ranked refiners by cost per unit of capacity. We then took the 10th and 90th percentiles of cost—corresponding to the second-lowest and second-highest cost estimates—and applied these to all refiners according to capacity, as measured in barrels per day.

As shown in Table 4.1, refiner cost estimates clustered between $9.00 and $37.00 per unit of production capacity. Two refiners produced higher estimates, one at $90 per unit and one at $187 per unit. We assume all of these to be good-faith estimates of refiner cost. Although some refiners might, in fact, face different costs because they would have more or less distance to go in order to meet the proposed requirements, a close reading of the survey responses indicates that this is not the major source of

Table 4.1
Capacity-Normalized, Refiner-Reported Costs

Refiner	Percentile	Unit Cost, in Dollars
A	0–8	9.33
B	8–17	9.61
C	17–25	9.74
D	25–33	18.39
E	33–42	20.90
F	42–50	21.58
G	50–58	26.98
H	58–67	27.18
I	67–75	36.72
J	75–83	36.73
K	83–92	90.00
L	92–100	186.72

variation in estimates. Instead, it appears that much of the variation stems from different inferences of how the regulations should be interpreted and how they might be enforced, with some refiners anticipating comparatively minor changes from current industry practice, while others anticipate extremely major changes.

To the extent that this is, in fact, the primary source of the variation among refiner estimates, we can expect the true cost of regulatory compliance to be more consistent across refineries. What that cost will be, however, is, at this point, unknown. We thus treat the variation in refiner estimates as a measure of the uncertainty of this final refiner cost. From this perspective, we can think of the numbers that the refiners actually reported as a "best" or average cost estimate. We take the 10th-percentile (second-lowest) and 90th-percentile (second-highest) estimates as the likely lower and upper bounds for this cost. Note that most estimates cluster near the lower end of this range, with much of the probability mass falling near the best estimate, in the range of $20 to $35 per unit.

Results

Summing costs from all refiners produces a best estimate of $58 million per year for refiners to maintain compliance with the proposed regulations. Using the technique described above, we calculate a range of $20 million per year on the low end and $183 million per year on the high end (see Table 4.2).

Figure 4.1 shows how these costs break out over the major PSM cost categories.

The largest cost categories are HCA at $12.7 million per year, DMR at $12.3 million per year, and RCA at $9.2 million per year. SPA and LOPA at $6.7 million per year, safety training at $3.2 million per year, PSCA at $2.9 million per year, and HFs at $2.9 million per year make up a second tier of cost in the range of $3 million per year to $7 million per year. PHA at $1 million per year, PM at $845,000 per year, and PIs at $400,000 per year make up a third tier of cost at or below $1 million per year industry wide. The other or undifferentiated cost category ($5.3 million per year) reflects primarily data that were reported in an aggregated form and cannot be broken

Table 4.2
Estimated Marginal Cost of
Regulatory Compliance, in Dollars

Estimate	Amount
Refiner-estimated total	57,571,983
Low	19,589,755
High	183,420,000

Figure 4.1
Estimated Annual Recurring Program Costs, in Dollars

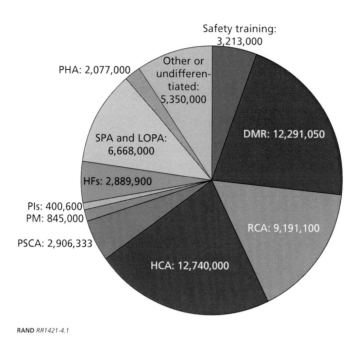

RAND *RR1421-4.1*

out into the stated categories without making unwarranted inferences—rather than actual costs not falling into the above-stated categories.

Estimates of Start-Up Costs

Whereas the estimates of most refiners were reasonably consistent with one another, several refiners anticipated costs that were much higher in certain categories. In some cases, we could determine that the anomalous numbers were the result of the respondent misunderstanding the question being asked—for instance, a report of the total cost of a program rather than the increase in that program's cost that might be attributed to the regulations. Problems of this sort were minimal, however, because of the extensive meetings to clarify the intent of the questions that we conducted before the refiners prepared their responses. In other cases, these answers—though anomalous— were within the bounds of the study: They did not seem to represent any kind of misunderstanding of the question; instead, they would seem to represent either a legitimate difference in the costs that certain refiners face or a legitimate difference in judgment with regard to how the regulations will be implemented and how much it might cost to comply with them. We have incorporated all answers regarding ongoing cost of compliance into the estimates presented here. Differences in opinion along these lines have been taken as a healthy part of the estimation process, and we leveraged them, using the techniques described above, to estimate a range of possible implementation costs.

Refiners estimated start-up costs less consistently, with some refiners providing minimal information, some providing estimates that combined start-up costs with ongoing costs for the first few years, and some clearly separating early-year operating costs from start-up costs. In virtually all cases, start-up costs were relatively small given the ongoing costs, ranging from 20 percent to 100 percent of one year's additional operating cost.

One refining company, however, estimates much higher expenses for the first five years of regulatory implementation with regard to the SPA and LOPA aspect of the regulation. This refining company, one of several refiners that operates two refineries in the state of California, estimates that the SPA and LOPA provisions of the regulations will cost its refineries an additional $300 million per year for each of the first five years across the two refineries ($200 million per year for one refinery and $100 million per year for the other). This is more than five times the total annual incremental cost that the entire industry projects in all sectors.

A large part of this refiner's projected cost would seem to stem from concern about the limits of applicability of the new regulations. This refiner reads the regulations as potentially applying extremely broadly, well beyond the boundaries of what are currently considered to be process safety issues. The refiner is also concerned that the corrective action item management regulations are overly prescriptive, possibly requiring all identified issues to be addressed with the same priority regardless of the level of risk posed. In particular, the refiner identified the SPA and LOPA regulations as applying to all possible failure scenarios rather than high-consequence failure scenarios with potential to cause a major incident. This refiner was further concerned with the use of the term *greatest extent feasible*, noting that it could be interpreted as "causing a company to focus on driving risks to near zero, at the expense of leaving 'moderate' hazard risk, which may have a greater process safety potential."

Most refiners did not see start-up costs as a major component of the costs of the proposed regulations, with most of the cost being the ongoing operational costs of running facilities as the new regulations would require. Under most refiners' estimates, the first one to five years could cost more than the following years by a factor of between 1.2 and 2 (with estimates tending toward the lower end of that range). If, however, the refiner discussed above is correct in its interpretation of the proposed regulatory environment and the costs of operating in that environment, the cost of the regulations over the first five years could be up to 20 times the ongoing cost estimated above.

CHAPTER FIVE

Major Incidents and Worker Deaths at California Refineries

Is there evidence that the proposed regulation will improve refinery safety and reduce worker fatalities and injuries? In this chapter, we examine historical data to determine whether past experience supports such a hypothesis.

First, we examine the characteristics and definition of *MRI*. PSM-related incidents at refineries can vary greatly in their size, damage done to the refinery, refinery-worker deaths and injuries, damage to nearby properties, and adverse health effects inflicted on residents of surrounding communities. In this report, we identify the characteristics of a prototypical MRI or a base case that can be used in subsequent economic analysis. We show that our base case falls in the middle of the range of possible MRIs.

Next, we review past refinery-worker deaths and identify trends in such fatalities under different refinery regulatory regimes. We calculate the probability of worker fatality in different regulatory regimes and examine the statistical significance of these results. Finally, we review MRIs that have occurred in California under two different regulatory regimes. In both cases, we estimate the probability of an MRI under each regulatory regime and examine the statistical significance of these results.

Definition of *Major Refinery Incident*

Until recently, there were no standard criteria for what constitutes an MRI. This changed in 2010. API developed process safety event (PSE) indicators in 2010 (API, 2010). Refinery operators can now submit PSE data to API in a standardized format that classifies PSEs into four categories, with tier 1 PSEs being the most severe. However, submission of the PSE data to API is voluntary on the part of refinery operators. Furthermore, we could not obtain any API reports containing summary PSE information for California refineries. In any case, the time period that the new API PSE standard covers is too short to be useful in the analysis needed here. This is because MRIs are rare events—only a few typically occur each decade. Because of the short time period for which data would theoretically be available, the information contained in the API database, even if there were 100-percent reporting by all California refineries, would be insufficient to provide statistically significant results.

Classification of Refinery Incidents

Local government offices, typically Certified Unified Program Agencies (CUPAs), keep records of hazardous material releases and other safety incidents that occur at California refineries. However, most CUPAs and Cal/OSHA or CalEPA regulators do not classify refinery incidents into major or minor incidents. CUPA refinery-incident records also include worker injuries or other reports that are not related to PSM issues. This lack of standardization within California makes it difficult to interpret the CUPA refinery-incident records. In addition, some CUPAs do not maintain refinery-incident records for long periods of time, leaving sizable reporting gaps for some refineries.

The one exception is Contra Costa Hazardous Materials Programs (CCHMP), which classifies MCARs into four categories or levels. CCHMP MCARs apply to refineries, as well as other facilities that process or store hazardous chemicals. During the 1990s, there was a series of MRIs in Contra Costa County, California. This led to regulatory changes governing refineries in the county, which we discuss in detail below. One outcome of these regulatory changes was the creation of a classification system for refinery incidents:

> Severity Level III—A fatality, serious injuries or major on-site and/or off-site damage occurred
>
> Severity Level II—An impact to the community occurred, or if the situation was slightly different the accident may have been considered major, or there is a recurring type of incident at that facility
>
> Severity Level I—A release where there was no or minor injuries, the release had no or slight impact to the community, or there was no or minor onsite damage
>
> Major Chemical Accident or Release (MCAR) is defined as:
>
> Major Chemical Accident or Release means an incident that meets the definition of a Level 3 or Level 2 incident in the Community Warning System incident level classification system defined in the Hazardous Materials Incident Notification Policy, as determined by Contra Costa Health Services; or results in the release of a regulated substance and meets one or more of the following criteria:
>
> - Results in one or more fatalities
> - Results in greater than 24 hours of hospital treatment of three or more persons
> - Causes on- and/or off-site property damage (including cleanup and restoration activities) initially estimated at $500,000 or more. On-site estimates

shall be performed by the regulated stationary source. Off-site estimates shall be performed by appropriate agencies and compiled by Health Services
- Results in a vapor cloud of flammables and/or combustibles that is more than 5,000 pounds[1]

Characteristics of Major Refinery Incidents

The definition of a level 3 MCAR above does not provide quantitative criteria that can be used to define *MRI*, nor does it provide information to estimate the economic consequences of the incident. Nor do the criteria provide a complete scope or context for what can take place in an MRI and its aftermath. We review past incidents to identify their salient characteristics.

Refinery Capacity and Outage Duration

Figure 5.1 shows two of several important parameters characterizing an MRI: the length of shutdown caused by the incident and the capacity of the refinery.

Some of the incidents shown are actual refinery incidents, while others, such as the Kern Oil incident, are hypothetical. The figure shows the Chevron Richmond Refinery fire of 2012 as a hypothetical incident. This incident did happen, but only part of the refinery was shut down, and for only nine months. The amount of gasoline

Figure 5.1
Capacity Losses from Major Refinery Incidents in California

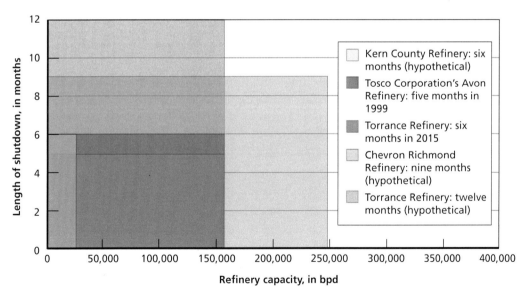

---

[1] Private communication with Randall Sawyer, director, CCHMP, February 2016.

production capacity lost in the incident is not known; Chevron has never divulged it.[2] So the lost production capacity shown in the figure for this incident is hypothetical and was likely less than that indicated in the figure.[3]

Figure 5.1 shows two ExxonMobil Torrance Refinery incidents. These refer to the same refinery and the same incident but differ in the duration of the refinery shutdown. At the time we concluded research for this study, the ExxonMobil Torrance Refinery had been shut down for six months; according to discussions with multiple refiners, very little, if any, gasoline was imported into the state of California during the first six months of the incident. We also know from discussions with regulators, as well as with ExxonMobil Torrance process safety experts, that gasoline production was almost entirely shut down for the first six months after the explosion at the refinery. The six-month ExxonMobil Torrance incident shown in the figure provides an accurate representation of the incident until June 2015. The refinery remained closed in the latter part of 2015 even though ExxonMobil appealed to regulators to permit gasoline production at the refinery using older pollution-control equipment. California regulators denied this request (Penn, 2015). ExxonMobil began to import specially produced batches of gasoline from overseas refineries capable of producing the California blend of reformulated gasoline or nearly finished California gasoline-blend components. Press reports indicate that the ExxonMobil Torrance Refinery will probably not reopen until early 2016 (Sider, 2015). For these reasons, we include a second ExxonMobil Torrance Refinery incident in the figure, which we label as hypothetical because the amount of lost production and the precise duration of the refinery outage cannot be determined at this time.

As we discuss later in this report, from an economic standpoint, lost gasoline production is an important result of an MRI. The area in each rectangle in the figure indicates the total amount of gasoline production lost during the entirety of each real or hypothetical refinery incident. If a small refinery is completely shut down because of an incident, the amount of production capacity lost will be relatively small even if the refinery is shut down for an extended period of time, as illustrated in the hypothetical Kern Oil case shown in the figure. On the other hand, if a large refinery suffers an incident, the amount of lost production capacity can be quite significant and can easily amount to 10 percent of the total gasoline production capacity in the state of California. Therefore, an important aspect of the MRI is what equipment and what processes the incident affects and whether the loss of these units shuts down gasoline production capacity or not.

---

[2]   We did ask for but could not obtain this information from Chevron.

[3]   In fact, the amount of production capacity lost in the Chevron refinery fire is probably significantly less than the refinery's maximum capacity (255,000 bpd) because Chevron was able to import intermediate-level feedstock into the refinery to continue some level of gasoline production.

Refinery-Worker Deaths

Another important characteristic of an MRI is whether workers die as a result of the incident. This is a criterion listed in both the API and CCHMP definitions of *MRI*. If any workers die as a result of an incident, both organizations classify the incident with the highest level of severity.

If there are fatalities, regulators can call for shutdown of the refinery until the root-cause investigation is complete and the refinery operator completes corrective actions to the regulator's satisfaction. This was the case in the 1999 Tosco refinery incident. During this incident, workers attempted repairs on a crude production unit while naphtha was leaking out of the system and while the unit was still in operation. The material ignited, causing a major fire and the deaths of four workers. The crude unit was then shut down, and repairs were made within a matter of days. Full production at the refinery was possible, and production capacity was restored at the refinery in a few days. But county leaders and regulators asked the refinery operator to shut down the refinery until all necessary corrective actions and a complete safety review could be completed.[4] This resulted in a five-month shutdown of the refinery, as indicated in the figure.

There were no worker fatalities in either the Chevron Richmond Refinery or ExxonMobil refinery incidents, although several workers were injured in the latter incident. In addition, in both cases, workers narrowly escaped much more-serious injury and possibly even death.

Analysts who have studied major industrial incidents that result in worker deaths identify incidents that cause multiple worker deaths as especially economically and psychologically damaging (Hopkins, 2015; Sunstein, 2004). Hopkins and (separately) Sunstein also discuss the concept that incidents causing multiple worker deaths have a much higher societal cost, which is why so much effort is made to prevent airline crashes. If the public were to lose confidence in the safety of airline travel because there are a few plane crashes in which most passengers are killed, the larger economic consequences could be very large and affect multiple sectors of the economy beyond the airline industry. In such a case, calculating all the indirect costs precisely would be difficult, but they could be quite large.

Fortunately, there have been no MRIs in California with multiple fatalities since the 1999 Tosco refinery incident. MRIs have, however, caused multiple deaths elsewhere in the United States. Table 5.1 shows examples of such incidents.

Adverse Health Effects on Nearby Residents

An MRI can also have adverse health effects on nearby residents. One result of the Chevron Richmond Refinery fire was that 15,000 nearby residents sought medical attention after the incident. Although there is no evidence that any nearby residents

---

[4]   The ISO was put into effect a month before the Tosco incident and gave CCHMP the ability to have a third-party perform a safety evaluation after an incident. The county hired Arthur D. Little to perform the evaluation.

Table 5.1
Major Refinery Incidents in the United States with Large
Numbers of Fatalities

Refinery Operator	Location	Incident Date	Fatalities
BP	Texas City, Texas	March 23, 2005	15
Union Oil	Romeoville, Ill.	July 23, 1984	19
Tesoro	Anacortes, Wash.	April 2, 2010	7
Shell Oil	Norco, La.	May 5, 1988	7

died as an immediate result of the incident, many suffered respiratory problems that required immediate medical attention.

CalARP requires all refineries in California and in the United States to develop and file RMPs with the state. In addition, the ISO requires refiners in Contra Costa County to submit safety plans (SPs) to CCHMP. These include descriptions of the worst-case hazardous chemical–release scenarios that could occur at each facility. Characteristics of these worst-case scenarios are the amount of hazardous chemicals released and the area to which they could spread beyond the facility itself. Some of the hazardous chemicals stored and used at refineries include ammonia, sulfuric acid, and hydrogen fluoride, as well as a host of hydrocarbon molecules that are hazardous to human health, including benzene. Fortunately, in MRIs that have occurred in California in the past couple of decades, the hazardous chemicals released have not led to the deaths of any nearby residents. Of course, one of the goals of PSM is to prevent incidents of this type from occurring. We were able to review the RMPs of many refineries operating in the state of California.[5] From this review, we were able to identify the most serious hazards and the worst-case scenarios associated with these facilities. Without going into sensitive details in this public report, it is sufficient to say that, in a worst-case scenario, hundreds of thousands of people in nearby communities could be seriously injured if a large release of the most hazardous chemicals were to occur. In these hypothetical events, tens or even hundreds of people could die as a direct result of the incident. Such a severe incident has never occurred at a U.S. refinery. Such a severe incident did occur at the Union Carbide plant in Bhopal, India. More than half a million people were reportedly injured, and thousands of people might have died. This represents an extreme and very rare case of a worst-case scenario actually occurring. In the economic analysis of MRIs that we describe later in this report, we do not make such a worst-case scenario the base case for analysis because such an incident has never occurred in the United States.

---

[5] The complete texts of RMPs are not posted online and are available for viewing at only a few locations. These precautions are taken to prevent terrorists from gaining knowledge of possible worst-case scenarios and where the most lethal chemicals are stored at refineries.

Notable Major Refinery Incidents in California

The above discussion shows that an MRI can be characterized by a relatively small number of key factors: the capacity of the refinery, the duration of the refinery outage resulting from the incident, the number of worker fatalities suffered in the incident, and the number of nearby residents injured or killed. History shows that an MRI can vary widely in its scope and economic impact depending on the size of these key factors. MRIs that have occurred in California over the past few decades are characterized by relatively few worker deaths but long refinery-outage periods. In a few cases, a large number of nearby residents have suffered significant adverse health effects, while, in others, the health of nearby residents has not been affected at all. We use these data to select a base case for MRIs for later economic analysis. Therefore, we define our base case as an incident in which no workers or nearby residents are killed.

Figure 5.1 shows three actual MRIs that resulted in major loss of gasoline production capacity: the 1999 Tosco incident, the 2012 Chevron refinery fire, and the 2015 ExxonMobil Torrance Refinery incident.

The Contra Costa County Industrial Safety Ordinance

As described briefly above, in the 1990s, there was a series of MRIs in Contra Costa County, California. This led to regulatory changes governing refineries in this one county. In this section, we investigate whether the more-stringent regulations adopted in Contra Costa County have resulted in fewer MRIs in Contra Costa County and fewer worker deaths than have occurred in the rest of the state.

Contra Costa County refineries have operated under the Contra Costa County ISO since January 1999, although its provisions were gradually applied and did not come into full effect until a year later—January 2000 (Contra Costa Health Services, 2014).

The Contra Costa County ISO is more stringent than the current refinery regulations under which other California refineries operate. In addition, although the proposed California refinery regulation is more stringent than the ISO, it bears a closer resemblance to the ISO and has less in common with current regulations.

The safety improvements that could result from the proposed regulation could reduce the number of future refinery incidents. If this happens, California refiners should suffer fewer major incidents. If this hypothesis is true, refineries that currently operate under the ISO might have suffered fewer major incidents than refineries that operate under current California regulations. In this chapter, we explore whether there is evidence to support this hypothesis.

Industrial Safety Ordinance and Non–Industrial Safety Ordinance Regulations and Refineries

Before we delve into incident history in detail, we review the changes in refinery regulation in Contra Costa County and in the city of Richmond because this history provides an important context for categorizing major refinery incidents. The county board of supervisors adopted the ISO on December 15, 1998, and the ISO went into effect in January 1999 (Contra Costa Health Services, 2014).

The city of Richmond adopted its own refinery regulation, called the Richmond ISO in 2002 (Contra Costa Health Services Hazardous Materials Program, 2011). From 2002 to 2006, the ISO and Richmond ISO contained similar regulatory guidance. The ISO was amended in 2006 to extend ISO requirements for facility HF programs to include maintenance and safety culture assessment. The revised ISO also expanded MOOC requirements to include maintenance and health and safety positions. It is important to note that the city of Richmond did not adopt these changes in 2006. It was not until after the Chevron Richmond Refinery fire of August 6, 2012, that the Richmond City Council adopted the ISO in full. On February 15, 2013, several months after the Chevron Richmond Refinery fire, the city council adopted the Contra Costa County ISO in its entirety (City of Richmond, 2013).

Given the above discussion, we can divide the set of California refineries into ISO refineries (those covered by the ISO) and non-ISO (NISO) refineries (not covered by the ISO). Table 5.2 lists the three ISO refineries that existed between 2000 and 2013.

Table 5.3 lists the nine NISO refineries that existed between 2000 and 2013. These include all California refineries outside of Contra Costa County and the Chevron Richmond Refinery.

As mentioned above, the Richmond city council adopted the Contra Costa County ISO in its entirety early in 2013. Shortly after 2013, the Chevron Richmond Refinery came under all the provisions of the ISO. Tables 5.4 and 5.5 reflect this change.

After 2013, California had the eight NISO refineries shown in Table 5.5. Finally, we note that all refineries in California that operated prior to 2000 should be consid-

Table 5.2
Industrial Safety Ordinance Refineries Between 2000 and 2013

Refinery	Owner	Location
Martinez	Shell	Martinez
Tesoro Martinez	Tesoro	Martinez
San Francisco	Phillips 66	Rodeo

Table 5.3
Non–Industrial Safety Ordinance Refineries Between 2000 and 2013

Refinery	Owner	Location
Chevron El Segundo	Chevron	El Segundo
Chevron Richmond	Chevron	Richmond
Torrance	ExxonMobil	Torrance
Kern County	Kern	Bakersfield
California	Paramount	Bakersfield, Long Beach, Paramount
Los Angeles	Phillips 66	Wilmington
Los Angeles	Tesoro	Carson
Valero Wilmington	Valero	Wilmington
Benicia	Valero	Benicia

Table 5.4
Industrial Safety Ordinance Refineries After 2013

Refinery	Owner	Location
Martinez	Shell	Martinez
Tesoro Martinez	Tesoro	Martinez
Chevron Richmond	Chevron	Richmond
San Francisco	Phillips 66	Rodeo

Table 5.5
Non–Industrial Safety Ordinance Refineries After 2013

Refinery	Owner	Location
Chevron El Segundo	Chevron	El Segundo
Torrance	ExxonMobil	Torrance
Kern County	Kern Oil	Bakersfield
Paramount Petroleum	Paramount	Bakersfield, Long Beach, Paramount
Los Angeles	Phillips 66	Wilmington
Los Angeles	Tesoro	Carson
Valero Wilmington	Valero	Wilmington
Benicia	Valero	Benicia

ered NISO refineries because, prior to 1999, the ISO did not exist, and, between 1999 and 2000, the ISO had not yet come fully into effect.

Refinery-Worker Deaths

Table 5.6 shows refinery incidents in California that resulted in the deaths of one or more refinery workers. This data set applies to MRIs that took place between 1995 and 2015 (Malewitz, Collette, and Olsen, 2015). To properly classify refinery-worker deaths and to remove worker fatalities from the public record that occurred at nonrefinery industrial facilities, in addition to using publicly available data, we used publicly unavailable information that Shell Oil U.S. and Tesoro supplied (Shell Martinez Refinery, 2016; Tesoro Refining and Marketing, 2016). We use these data to investigate the question of whether refinery-worker fatalities are lower in ISO refineries than in NISO refineries.

Public information indicates that a single death occurred in an ISO refinery (not shown in Table 5.6). This was an incident at Shell's Martinez Refinery in Martinez, California, on August 20, 2009 (Malewitz, Collette, and Olsen, 2015). In this incident, there was no release of hazardous chemicals and no fire. In this case, a refinery worker drowned in a freshwater tank. The investigation concluded that the incident was not work related. This was not considered a process safety incident because the water tank was equipped with a railing to prevent accidents and was not a covered process component at the time of the incident. In addition, there is evidence, as mentioned, that the death was not work related (Shell Martinez Refinery, 2016). As a consequence, CCHMP did not record this worker fatality event as an MCAR event.

Every MRI that resulted in a fatality occurred at a NISO refinery. A total of 15 workers died at NISO refineries, while no worker died at an ISO refinery during the time period under consideration.

Using these data, one can calculate the probability that a refinery worker will die at an ISO refinery in a yearlong period. We call this $P_{wd}(ISO)$. It equals the total number of refinery-worker deaths at ISO refineries in the specified time period (n_wd_ISO) divided by the total number of years in which refineries that were subject to the ISO operated. We call the latter number ISO refinery-years, which we label n_ryr_ISO.

A similar refinery-worker fatality probability can be computed for NISO refineries, which we call $P_{wd}(NISO)$.

One finds that

$$P_{wd}(ISO) = \frac{n\_wd\_ISO}{n\_ryr\_ISO} = \frac{0}{51} = 0,$$

Table 5.6
California Refinery-Worker Deaths

Original Refinery Name	Current Refinery Name	Number of Deaths	PSM Event	Incident Date	ISO Refinery?
BP	Tesoro Los Angeles	1	No	June 22, 2011	NISO
Shell Oil	Martinez	0[a]	No	April 29, 2009	ISO
ExxonMobil Torrance	ExxonMobil Torrance	1	Yes	April 11, 2009	NISO
ConocoPhillips	Phillips 66 Los Angeles	1	Yes	April 10, 2006	NISO
ExxonMobil Torrance	ExxonMobil Torrance	1	Yes	September 14, 2005	NISO
Kern Oil and Refining	Kern Oil and Refining	1	Yes	January 19, 2005	NISO
Equilon Enterprises LLC	Tesoro Los Angeles	0[b]	No	June 11, 2004	NISO
ExxonMobil	ExxonMobil Torrance	1	Yes	April 3, 2003	NISO
ExxonMobil	ExxonMobil Torrance	1	Yes	February 22, 2001	NISO
Tosco Avon	Tesoro Martinez	4	Yes	February 23, 1999	NISO
Arco	Tesoro Los Angeles	1	No	August 20, 1998	NISO
Tosco Avon	Tesoro Martinez	1	Yes	January 21, 1997	NISO
Unocal	Phillips 66 Santa Maria	1	Yes	September 7, 1995	NISO

SOURCES: Malewitz, Collette, and Olsen, 2015; Tesoro Refining and Marketing, 2016; Shell Martinez Refinery, 2016.

[a] A refinery worker drowned in a freshwater tank. There was no evidence that he was exposed to hazardous chemicals at the time of his death. Evidence does exist that his death was not work related. Therefore, we remove this fatality from the data, as indicated by the 0 for this incident for the number of deaths.

[b] A refinery worker collapsed and died while on the refinery premises. There was no evidence that he was exposed to hazardous chemicals at the time of death. It was later determined that he died of a heart attack. For this reason, we remove this one fatality from the data, as indicated by the zero for this incident under number of deaths.

and the NISO probability of worker death is

$$P_{wd}(NISO) = \frac{n\_wd\_NISO}{n\_ryr\_NISO} = \frac{14}{201} = 0.07.$$

The variables in the above equations have the same meaning for NISO refineries as they do for ISO refineries.

Both statistical groups or populations can be appropriately described by binomial distributions. For n large enough (more than 200), we can approximate key statistical measures of the binomial distribution by the normal distribution (this holds in the NISO case but not for the ISO case) (Rosner, 2015). We can employ the normal approximation to determine the confidence interval (CI) around the NISO probability estimate. We can use this approximation because of the large number of refinery-years or samples available for the NISO case (201 refinery-years). The normal approximation reveals the CI to be 0.034 to 0.10.

There are not enough samples to employ the normal approximation to the ISO data set (only 51 refinery-years). However, we can use the NISO CI for the NISO data set and compare it with the ISO probability estimate (0.0). P_{wd} (ISO) lies outside the NISO CI. So we can conclude that it is unlikely to belong to the same statistical population. Therefore, we can conclude that the statement $P_{wd}(ISO) < P_{wd}(NISO)$ is likely to be true. The probability of a refinery-worker death in a *NISO* refinery is substantially larger than that for an ISO refinery.

Industrial Safety Ordinance Refinery-Incident History

Figure 5.2 shows the MCARs that have taken place in Contra Costa County since the ISO was enacted. CCHMP tracks MCARs each year and reports these to the public in its annual performance report. CCHMP also maintains a website that has data on Contra Cost County–regulated entities' incident histories that lists the incident, incident description, and the facility where the incident occurred.

Figure 5.2
Industrial Safety Ordinance Refinery Major Chemical Accidents and Releases Between 1999 and 2014

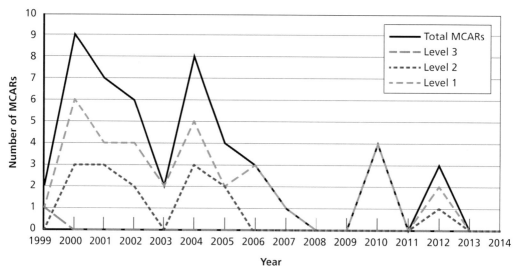

SOURCE: Contra Costa Health Services, undated.
AND *RR1421-5.2*

Figure 5.2 shows that there has been only one level 3 MCAR since the ISO was enacted in Contra Costa County. This was the Tosco refinery incident that occurred in 1999 after the ISO was enacted but before Contra Costa County had to come into compliance with the regulation. In fact, the Tosco refinery incident took place a little more than a month after the ISO came into force but 11 months before Contra Costa County refineries were required to deliver their SPs that described how each facility would come into compliance with the regulation. Because Contra Costa County refineries covered under the ISO had not yet implemented all aspects of the ISO in early 1999, we exclude this incident from the ISO data set.

We conclude that, since the ISO was enacted and implemented, there has been only MRI under the ISO, the accidental drowning of a refinery worker at the Shell Martinez Refinery in 2009.

Non–Industrial Safety Ordinance Refinery-Incident History

Identifying MRIs that have occurred in NISO refineries is more difficult because the relevant CUPAs do not classify refinery incidents or publish reports that contain this information. In addition, CUPAs outside of Contra Costa County do not require refinery operators to include all significant refinery incidents that have occurred in the past ten to 15 years in their RMPs. RMPs include data only on MRIs that have occurred in the five years prior to publication. In contrast, CCHMP lists all significant refinery incidents that have occurred since the 1990s in its SPs.[6]

Nevertheless, NISO-refinery RMPs can be used to determine whether an MRI has occurred in the five years prior to RMP publication. The Chevron Richmond Refinery incident is included in the most recent SP that Chevron Richmond Refinery published in 2013. The ExxonMobil Torrance Refinery incident, however, is too recent and is not included in the most recent RMP for this facility. We reviewed as many RMPs and SPs as possible and used the RMP and SP data available to the public from "The Right-to-Know Network" (Center for Effective Government, undated) to identify other possible refinery incidents that could have released large amounts of hazardous chemicals into the air and caused adverse health effects off-site (thereby constituting an MRI). In addition, we used data available from CCHMP and that Randall Sawyer cited in his testimony to Congress that includes MRIs that occurred in Contra Costa County prior to 1999 (Sawyer, 2013). We extended our analysis of major incidents at California refineries back to 1994, based on data available from CCHMP. RMP records obviously do not extend that far back in time, so we have to rely on other records.

---

[6] Refiner SPs closely resemble RMPs.

Table 5.7 lists known NISO MRIs. The table includes the two confirmed major incidents in which the off-site effects were so significant that they are well known, the Chevron Richmond and ExxonMobil Torrance refinery incidents. In fact, drivers in the state of California were feeling the effects of the latter refinery incident in June 2015: The price of gasoline has remained significantly higher in California than elsewhere in the United States. Later in this report, we show that this price difference is the result of this refinery incident.

Using the data above, one can calculate the annual probability that an MRI will occur at an ISO refinery using the same approach used in calculating the probability of refinery-worker death. We call this $P_{MRI}(ISO)$. The ISO data set is essentially the same, and the same result holds.

The probability for NISO refineries is $P_{MRI}(ISO) = 0$.

In this case, we can use CCHMP data to extend the data set for NISO refinery incidents back to 1992. Then the probability of an MRI at any of the NISO refineries in California in a given year is $P_{MRI}(NISO) = 0.066$.

We can employ the normal approximation to determine the CI around the NISO probability estimate. We can use this approximation because of the large number of

Table 5.7
Major Incidents at Non–Industrial Safety Ordinance Refineries

Refinery Operator at Time of Incident	Location	Worker Death?	Date
ExxonMobil	Torrance	No	February 15, 2015
Chevron	Richmond	No	August 5, 2012
BP	Tesoro Los Angeles	Yes	June 22, 2011
ExxonMobil	Torrance	Yes	April 11, 2009
ConocoPhillips	P66 Wilmington	Yes	April 10, 2006
ExxonMobil	Torrance	Yes	September 14, 2005
Kern Oil and Refining	Bakersfield	Yes	January 19, 2005
ExxonMobil	Torrance	Yes	April 3, 2003
ExxonMobil	Torrance	Yes	February 22, 2001
Tosco Avon	Tesoro Martinez	Yes	February 23, 1999
Arco	Tesoro Los Angeles	Yes	August 20, 1998
Tosco Avon	Tesoro Martinez	Yes	January 21, 1997
Unocal	Nipomo	Yes	September 7, 1995
Unocal	Rodeo	No	August 22, 1994

SOURCES: Center for Effective Government, undated; refinery RMPs and SPs; Chevron USA, 2013; Malewitz, Collette, and Olsen, 2015.

refinery-years or samples available for the NISO case (237 refinery-years). The normal approximation reveals the CI to be 0.032 to 0.094.

We cannot use the normal approximation to determine the CI for P_{MRI} (ISO) because of the small size of n (only 51 refinery-years).

However, one can use the NISO CI for the NISO data set and compare it with the ISO probability estimate (0.0). The mean for the ISO data sample lies outside of the NISO CI, so one can conclude that it is unlikely to belong to the same statistical population. One can also calculate the one-sample inference method for the binomial distribution to determine that the ISO data sample is not consistent with the hypothesis that it belongs to the NISO distribution (Rosner, 2015, p. 244). Therefore, we can conclude that the statement $P_{MRI}(ISO) < P_{MRI}(NISO)$ is likely to be true. The probability of an MRI in a *NISO* refinery is substantially larger than that for an ISO refinery.

Costly Major Refinery Incidents

The above analysis estimates the probabilities of an MRI or worker death for refineries in California operating under the ISO or outside of the ISO regulatory regime. The above estimates are for an MRI, as defined by the API or CCHMP. However, many of these incidents do not lead to major economic losses for the refiner or for California consumers. Only a small subset of MRIs turns out to have a major impact on the state economy. The analysis in the next chapter shows that the largest economic impact of an MRI is lost gasoline production, and this occurs only if a refinery is completely or partially shut down for a substantial period of time after the incident—so that a large amount of gasoline is removed from the California gasoline market. In many MRIs, the refinery is not shut down, and there is no lost production.

We define *CMRI* as an incident that has a major impact on the California economy. By *costly*, we mean that the incident that results in a macroeconomic impact of $1.5 billion or more. The analysis presented below indicates there have been only three such incidents in California in the past 16 years. These are the three notable MRIs mentioned earlier: the Tosco refinery incident of 1999, the Chevron Richmond incident of 2012, and the ExxonMobil Torrance refinery incident of 2015.

CHAPTER SIX

Impact of Major Refinery Incidents on California Gasoline Prices

In this chapter, we examine MRIs' impact on the price of gasoline in the state of California. To conduct this analysis, we build a model that can be used to predict the price of gasoline in California. We use the model and historical price data from past MRIs to determine how much of the change in the price of gasoline during the refinery outage is due to the refinery incident.

U.S. Gasoline Prices

As discussed in Chapter One, the California gasoline market is isolated from the market in the rest of the United States. A premium is paid for California gasoline because of the unique California formulation requirements for gasoline and because large-scale pipelines do not exist from the eastern United States into California. Nevertheless, the U.S. price of gasoline is correlated with the California price because both products depend on the same input material—crude oil—and because crude oil prices in California and the rest of the United States are, for the most part, set by the price of oil at storage facilities located at Cushing, Oklahoma. This U.S. market price for oil is referred to as the price of West Texas Intermediate.

We use this correlation to build a California gas price model that we use to predict gas prices. To do this, we use past prices to set key parameters in the model.

Figure 6.1 shows the close correlation of U.S. and California gas prices. We take care, however, to exclude past periods of time when other market or economic effects could affect the correlation. Given there have been structural changes in the market in the past 15 years, we focus on January 1, 2011, to the present with removal of two known large incidents. This is designated as the analysis window in Figure 6.1.

Gasoline Price Model

To assess the impact that large-scale refinery incidents can have on the price of gasoline in California, we estimate the average weekly price of California gasoline based on the

Figure 6.1
California Versus U.S. Gasoline Prices

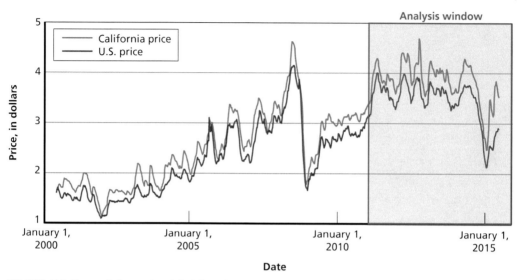

SOURCE: U.S. Energy Information Administration.
RAND RR1421-6.1

average U.S. price of gasoline. To control for the potential differences in the refining process for summer and winter gasoline, we also used seasonal variables. Because of the large-scale economic downturn that began in 2008 and was reflected in gas prices through 2010, we collected data for January 2011 through June 2015 from the U.S. Energy Information Administration for both the weekly average U.S. price of gasoline and the weekly average California price of gasoline. Additionally, we removed data for the six months after the Chevron Richmond incident and all of 2015 so we could understand the relationship between U.S. and California gasoline prices when California operations were acting under "normal" conditions.

We regressed the weekly U.S. gasoline prices on weekly California gasoline prices with the associated seasonal effects using ordinary least squares. A mathematical representation for this regression is given by

$$P_{CAL,t} = \alpha P_{US,t} + \sum_{i=2}^{12} \beta_i I_i(t) + \varepsilon_t,$$

where $P_{CAL,t}$ is the price of gasoline in California and $P_{US,t}$ is the price of gasoline in the United States; $I_i(t)$ is an indicator function that takes the value 1 if the observation is in month i and 0 otherwise; ε_t is a normally distributed error term; and α and β_t are coefficients to be estimated. The resulting estimation explains 98 percent of the variance in the California gasoline prices ($R^2 = 0.98$). From this estimation, we can predict California gasoline prices for the entire time from January 2011 to June 2015 based on the estimated coefficients and the realized U.S. gasoline prices. The predicted gasoline prices are in the absence of any disruptions within the California market. The difference between the actual California gasoline price and the predicted gasoline price in the six months following a disruption in capacity is an estimate of the disruption's impact on gasoline prices.

Figure 6.2 shows the predicted gas price and actual California gas prices for the analysis time period. It shows that the price of gasoline diverged significantly from the predicted price during the two MRIs that occurred in the analysis time. In the next section, we examine in detail these price differences.

Impact on Refinery Incidents on California Gas Prices

2012 Chevron Richmond Refinery Incident

Between 2011 and 2015, there have been two MRIs in California. The first incident is the Chevron Richmond Refinery fire that broke out on August 12, 2012. The fire was started under piping connected to the crude-distillation unit. The crude-distillation unit suffered significant damage, which took time to repair. In addition, Cal/OSHA, CalEPA, and the CSB investigated the incident. These investigations took time to complete to definitively determine the cause of the incident. Regulators also needed

Figure 6.2
Predicted Versus Actual California Gasoline Prices

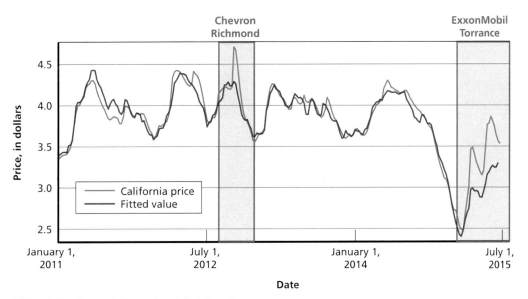

SOURCE: U.S. Energy Information Administration.
RAND RR1421-6.2

additional time to determine whether the repairs and other remedies that Chevron put in place would prevent a similar type of incident in the future.

Consequently, the crude-distillation unit was not restarted until April 25, 2013 (about a month earlier, Chevron was given permission to restart the unit). One could assume that gasoline production had to be completely stopped at the refinery between August 12, 2012, and April 25, 2013. However, this is not the case. Chevron was able to import intermediate feedstock that other refineries (probably located outside of California) produced and so was able to resume some amount of gasoline production at the Chevron Richmond Refinery shortly after the fire.[1] And at the same time, the delivery of crude oil to the refinery was probably stopped.

Figure 6.3 shows the impact that the Chevron Richmond Refinery incident had on California gas prices. We see that, immediately after the incident, there was a spike in California gas prices. This first spike in prices meant that California consumers had to pay $117 million more for gasoline than if the refinery incident had not occurred. After this initial price spike, California and U.S. gas prices closely track one another until about October 2012. Then another significant price spike occurs. The second gas price spike was larger and cost California consumers $330 million.

Because internal refinery operations and production numbers are considered to be highly proprietary, Chevron was not willing to share gasoline production changes at the Chevron Richmond Refinery with us. Therefore, we cannot with absolute certainty

Figure 6.3
Impact That the Chevron Richmond Refinery Incident Had on California Gas Prices

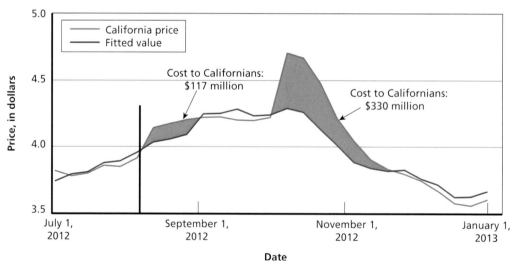

SOURCE: U.S. Energy Information Administration.
RAND RR1421-6.3

---

[1]   Private communication from a Chevron representative, May 13, 2015.

attribute the spike in gas prices to gasoline production losses at the Chevron refinery. However, it is plausible to say that, after an initial spike in gas prices, Chevron was able to contract intermediate-level feedstock for delivery to the refinery. Then, for some reason, perhaps because of lack of availability of feedstock or other refineries going off-line to switch from summer to winter blends, there was an additional price spike. The second spike in gas prices ended by the middle of November. It could be that, at that time, Chevron was able to put in place long-term contracts for intermediate-level feedstock that enabled the Chevron refinery to operate at full production capacity for gasoline.

Despite the uncertainty regarding how much production capacity the Chevron Richmond Refinery lost as a result of the incident, we can estimate the additional cost California consumers had to pay for gasoline as a result of this incident. Figure 6.3 shows the total added cost to California consumers of the Chevron Richmond refinery incident to be approximately $447 million.

2015 ExxonMobil Torrance Refinery Incident

On February 18, 2015, an explosion in a gasoline processing unit occurred at the ExxonMobil refinery in Torrance, California. Four workers suffered minor injuries in this incident, and debris from the explosion was dispersed into the surrounding community. The Torrance fire department advised local residents with health issues, the elderly, and children to shelter in place and for residents to shut down air-conditioning units. Children at local schools were told to shelter in place for several hours. The fire department recommended that the same precautions be taken at city facilities. It was quickly determined that the electrostatic precipitator (ESP), a pollution-control device, had exploded and spread metallic and silica-based catalysts used inside the system into the surrounding community (Rocha, 2015a).

The CSB is still investigating the root cause of this incident and has not published its findings. Press reports indicate that a hydrocarbon release from the fluid catalytic cracker unit into the ESP caused the blast. The hydrocarbon release caused the ESP to explode. After the incident, Cal/OSHA ordered ExxonMobil to shut down the unit until it could demonstrate safe operation (Rocha, 2015b). From the time of the explosion in February to August 2015, the refinery has remained shut down and gasoline production stopped.

The ExxonMobil Torrance Refinery has a production capacity of 155,000 bpd. This amount of gasoline was immediately taken off the market after this incident. Figure 6.4 shows the estimated impact of this incident in terms of increased gas prices.

The figure shows that, up until the beginning of July 2015, the ExxonMobil Torrance Refinery incident's cost to California consumers has been more than $2.4 billion. If this incident could have been avoided, California consumers would not have had to pay the higher costs for gasoline shown in the figure.

Figure 6.4
Impact That the ExxonMobil Torrance Refinery Incident Had on California Gas Prices

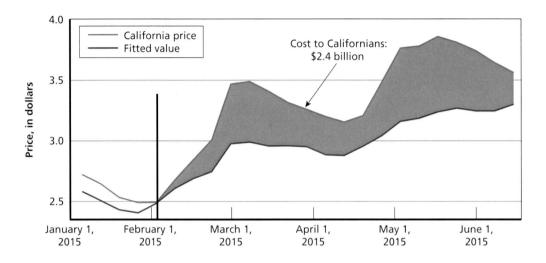

SOURCE: U.S. Energy Information Administration.
RAND RR1421-6.4

CHAPTER SEVEN

Macroeconomic Impact Estimates

Macroeconomic Impact Analysis

As described in Chapter Three, we used the IMPLAN model to assess the secondary, macroeconomic impacts on the California economy of both the cost of the proposed regulations and the cost (to be avoided) of an MRI. As context for this analysis, we note that IMPLAN estimates the current value of the output of the California petroleum-refining sector at $131 billion per year, making it the fourth-largest industry by output in the state. Approximately 90 percent of the industry's revenue goes to cover inputs (primarily crude oil). The remaining 10 percent, as estimated by IMPLAN, is divided into about 7 percent return to capital and 3 percent return to labor (e.g., wages, salaries).

As further context, we note that the estimated cost of the proposed regulations, although substantial in absolute terms, is small for the size of the industry. The best estimate of $58 million is only 0.04 percent of industry revenue not devoted to inputs and about 0.005 percent of industry revenue overall.

IMPLAN estimates total compensation in the California refinery sector to be about $334,000 per employee. The best estimate of $58 million in additional labor costs therefore implies the creation of about 158 jobs in the petroleum-refining sector if the major source of costs is additional labor (with a range of 57 to 325 jobs).

We model the regulations' impact on the refining sector as a shift from capital to labor with no resulting change in output. This produces a very modest indirect and induced impact on the California economy of about ten (low: 3.5, high: 31) additional jobs earning an additional $590,000 (low: $200,000; high: $1,850,000) and adding another $1.15 million (low: $400,000; high: $3.6 million) in value added for a total induced impact on the California economy of an additional $1.86 million in gross domestic product (low $640,000; high: $5.85 million).

We estimated the price impact of the proposed regulations separately under the assumptions that additional regulatory costs will be passed on to consumers through increased gasoline prices and that demand for gasoline is perfectly inelastic. In recent years, gasoline consumption in California has averaged about 14.5 billion gallons per year. Spreading the $58 million estimated cost of the regulations across this volume of sales indicates an increase in price of about $0.004 per gallon. The lower estimate of $20 million moves this impact down to $0.0014, while the upper estimate of $183 million moves the impact up to $0.013 per gallon.

Aggregating this up to calculate the impact on the average adult Californian gives an estimated cost per person of about $2 per year, with a low estimate of $0.68 and a high estimate of $6.20 per person per year.

Macroeconomic Impact of a Major Refinery Incident

Turning to the benefit side of the equation, we use IMPLAN to examine the secondary macroeconomic costs of an MRI. ExxonMobil Torrance and Chevron Richmond are two plausible scenarios from history that we can use to assess the macroeconomic impacts on the California economy as a whole. In addition, these might not be the worst incidents that have the potential to occur. As such, we consider potential shutdowns ranging in duration, as well as the size of plant that incurs the shutdown. The refineries in California range in capacity from 25,000 bpd to 377,000 bpd. We also consider a range of shutdown durations from three months to one year. Seven of the 12 refineries produce roughly 150,000 bpd. Given the linearity of the IMPLAN model, the impacts of any scenario are multiplicative based on relative impacts. For example, the impact of a shutdown of a 150,000-bpd plant for 12 months is twice the impact of shutting it down for six months in all categories of impacts. Our base impact is to consider a 150,000-bpd refinery being shut down for six months. This corresponds to an 8-percent reduction in output for the refining industry statewide over six months, or the equivalent of a 4-percent reduction in output over the course of a year. We classify the impacts of this incident in terms of employment (number of full-time–equivalent jobs), labor income (payroll for those jobs), proprietor income (payments to capital), and impact on overall output (GSP). We also break out these effects in terms of the direct effect (value of lost production), indirect effect (impact of that lost production as inputs from and to other sectors), and induced effect (changes in demand as a result of lost income to employees and capital owners) as the shock ripples through the other sectors of the economy. The estimated impacts of this scenario are summarized as follows.

This analysis indicates that the overall impact that such an incident has on the state of California is much larger than either the price impact on consumers at $2.4 billion (as estimated in the previous chapter) or the value of the lost supply of nearly $5 billion (4 percent of the value of annual output). The total impact that an incident on the scale of the recent one at ExxonMobil Torrance, as estimated with the IMPLAN model, could have on California GSP is about $7 billion. Similarly, the direct loss of 480 jobs (which, in practice, additional maintenance and repair activity might offset) is small for the estimated macroeconomic impact, which is estimated to cost 8,720 jobs.

To summarize the potential impacts that an alternative-size major incident could have on the California economy, we construct alternative scenarios. In our base scenario, annual output in the refining sector was reduced by 4 percent. As alternatives, we also consider 1 percent, 2 percent, 8 percent, and 10 percent (see Table 7.1). These output reductions can come about by either the size of the refinery affected or the duration of the shutdown. For example, an 8-percent reduction in annual supply can arise from either a 150,000-bpd refinery shutting down for 12 months or a 300,000-bpd refinery shutting down for six months. As such, we express the shutdown in terms of disruptions to aggregate annual supply loss. Table 7.2 summarizes these impacts and, in the last column, gives a multiplier that can be used to transform the impacts in Table 7.1 to the particular scenario. Table 7.2 expresses only the total impact and not the direct, indirect, or induced.

The size of the expected benefit from reducing the probability of such an incident depends heavily on how much we can expect the regulations to reduce this probability.

We can use this analysis to estimate the total macroeconomic impact of the three costly major incidents that have occurred in the state of California in the past two decades. Here, we are interested in the potential impact that these incidents could have on the current California economy, with its isolated gasoline market and current

Table 7.1
Macroeconomic Impact of a Costly Major Incident, Such as ExxonMobil's in 2015

Impact Type	Employment	Labor Income, in Dollars	Proprietor Income, in Dollars	Output (GSP), in Dollars
Direct effect	−480	−165,000,000	−363,000,000	−4,924,000,000
Indirect effect	−4,740	−393,000,000	−235,000,000	−1,514,000,000
Induced effect	−3,500	−182,000,000	−130,000,000	−510,000,000
Total effect	−8,720	−740,000,000	−728,000,000	−6,948,000,000

Table 7.2
Alternative Scenarios of Major Impacts

Scenario (Output Reduction)	Employment	Labor Income, in Dollars	Proprietor Income, in Dollars	Output (GSP), in Dollars	Multiplier
1%	−2,180	−185,000,000	−182,000,000	−1,737,000,000	0.25
2%	−4,360	−370,000,000	−364,000,000	−3,474,000,000	0.50
4%	−8,720	−740,000,000	−728,000,000	−6,948,000,000	1.00
8%	−17,440	−1,480,000,000	−1,465,000,000	−13,896,000,000	2.00
10%	−21,800	−1,850,000,000	−1,820,000,000	−17,370,000,000	2.50

economic structure. Because the ExxonMobil Torrance 2015 and Chevron Richmond 2012 incidents occurred recently, we expect that this estimate will be close to the actual cost. In the case of Tosco 1999, we estimate not the cost of the incident when it occurred but the impact that such an incident would have on the California economy if it were to happen today.

Using the calculations developed in Table 7.2, and having good estimates of lost production for each of these incidents (documented in Chapter Eight), we can estimate the total losses for all three of these costly major incidents. ExxonMobil Torrance 2015 produced a loss of approximately 27.8 million barrels, Tosco 1999 a loss of 16.5 million barrels, and Chevron Richmond 2012 a loss of 6.9 million barrels. As demonstrated above, the cost to the California economy of the ExxonMobil loss was approximately $6.95 billion. Using the IMPLAN analysis outlined in Table 7.2, we can estimate the economic impact of the Tosco loss at about $4.11 billion (if it were to happen today) and the Chevron Richmond loss at about $1.72 billion.

Taken together, these three costly major incidents constitute a loss of $12.78 billion to the California economy over the 16 years between 1999 and 2015. We can restate this as an expected annual loss of $12.78 billion ÷ 16, or $800 million per year (rounding $798.5 million). We take this to be a good estimate of the expected annual cost of such incidents under the current regulatory system.

CHAPTER EIGHT

Potential Benefits to Industry

The safety improvements that might result from the proposed regulation could reduce the number of future refinery incidents. If this is the case, refiners that implement the measures called for in the proposed regulation should suffer fewer major incidents. Under this hypothesis, industry will avoid the costs that such incidents impose, and the proposed regulation will provide a benefit to industry in terms of avoidance of these costs. In Chapter Nine, we explore whether there is evidence that this hypothesis is indeed true.

Refiners that suffer major incidents can incur a variety of different types of costs as a result of the incident:

- equipment repair costs
- workers' compensation
- fines
- nearby residents' health care costs
- emergency response costs
- lost profit from reduced production.

Costs incurred included costs to repair equipment that was damaged during the incident. Another cost might be workers' compensation payments for workers who are injured in the incident and who later cannot work for some period of time. As a result of the incident, refiners might be fined for violating existing regulations. In addition, in a major incident, residents of nearby communities could suffer adverse health effects, so the refiner might be obligated to pay health care costs for these residents. The refiner might also be liable for the costs that emergency response units incur, especially if the incident required a large-scale and extended emergency response from local police and fire departments. Finally, the refiner might have to shut down production for some period of time, so refinery profits during the refinery shutdown period might be partially or completely eliminated (depending on what part of the refinery is damaged and where the incident occurs in the refinery).

Consequently, the benefits to refiners of avoiding MRIs are complex and might be difficult to estimate because refiners consider relevant cost data proprietary. In addition, these costs could differ significantly from one major incident to another. We discuss these costs, and what we could learn about them, for three recent refinery incidents.

ExxonMobil Torrance Refinery Incident of 2015

Repair Costs

ExxonMobil was unwilling to provide us with the cost to repair equipment that was damaged or found to be unsafe after the Torrance Refinery incident in 2015. Such information is highly sensitive and proprietary for refiners. In addition, the incident investigation was still ongoing when we finished this study, so a final determination of the cause of the incident might not have been determined by July 2015. Until the cause is determined, determining the final repair costs incurred in this incident might not be possible.

Fines

Refiners might also be subject to fines that regulators impose after such incidents. ExxonMobil was recently fined $566,000 in conjunction with the 2015 incident. The CSB investigation into the cause of the incident continues. So regulators might levy additional fines in this case. When compared with the lost revenues and cost of repairs, however, the cost of regulatory fines is insignificant, coming in at little more than 0.01 percent of the lost proprietor income.

The lost income and fines above, plus the cost of repairing the facility, would be the short-term economic cost to the refiner for the incident. Conceived in more-general terms, it is plausible to say that an incident of this scale could cost a refiner something on the order of half a billion dollars once repair costs are included.

Nearby Residents' Health Care Costs

Health care costs that nearby residents incurred in the Torrance incident have apparently been minimal. That spent catalyst that was released in the explosion of the ESP fell on nearby homes and automobiles. We could not find any reports of major health problems of nearby residents.

Emergency Response Costs

We could not ascertain the emergency response costs that Torrance fire and police departments incurred during the incident or how much of this cost ExxonMobil has paid.

Production Profit Losses

We can, however, estimate the losses from such incidents by looking at the value of the product that is not produced. To do this, we examine a stylized version of the ExxonMobil Torrance incident of 2015. This facility is rated at 155,000 bpd. At $4 per gallon, its output for six months is worth about $4.7 billion. IMPLAN data indicate that 90 percent of refiner revenue is spent to cover inputs—primarily crude oil—and these expenditures did not need to be made while the plant was off-line. Also according to IMPLAN, the remaining 10 percent of revenue (the value added) can be divided into 3 percent labor income and 7 percent proprietor income. Proprietor income can further be divided between capital depreciation and profit. However, depreciation can be expected to proceed during downtime, so it is not reduced in the same way that feedstock and labor are reduced. Thus, 7 percent is a good estimate of actual economic loss to the refiner. In the ExxonMobil case, this comes to $332 million for a six-month refinery outage.

Chevron Richmond Refinery Incident of 2012

On the afternoon of August 6, 2012, a hydrocarbon leak from piping connected to the 4 Crude Unit caught fire. It took several hours to bring the fire under control. A shelter-in-place order was issued, affecting approximately 55,000 people, which advised residents to remain indoors until the fire was controlled. At 11:12 p.m., the shelter-in-place order was lifted. Approximately 15,000 people sought medical attention as a result of exposure to the hazardous smoke plume from the fire. Six employees received first aid as a result of the incident, but there were no injuries (Chevron USA, 2013).

Repair Costs

Chevron was also unwilling to provide us with the final costs to repair equipment that was damaged or found to be unsafe after the Richmond Refinery incident in 2012. It should be noted that, in February 2013, Chevron estimated these costs to be $5.3 million (Chevron USA, 2013). However, repair costs might have been greater than this amount because regulators might have required additional repairs and changes before approving start-up of the damaged crude unit.

Fines

Press reports indicate that Chevron was fined $1.28 million for violating safety regulations and $145,600 for violating air-quality regulations (Cagle, 2013).

Nearby Residents' Health Care Costs

Chevron reported to local regulators that, as of January 21, 2013, 23,900 claims had been initiated as a result of the Richmond Refinery incident. Chevron reported that it had provided approximately $10 million in compensation to area hospitals, affected community team members with valid claims, and local government agencies. As described below, the majority of the claims that Chevron paid are for health care costs.

Emergency Response Costs

Contra Costa County charged Chevron approximately $60,000 to compensate for overtime and other salary costs that county emergency response teams incurred as a result of the incident.[1]

It should be noted that Contra Costa County did not charge Chevron for all county agency follow-up costs beyond the time involved with responding to the immediate incident. County officials spent hundreds of hours following up on the incident, preparing presentations and working public meetings, and working with a third party to do a safety evaluation. The contract for the safety evaluations is for $876,600.[2]

Production Profit Loses

There is more uncertainty in the estimated cost to the refiner of the Chevron Richmond incident of 2012 because Chevron did not have to shut down all gasoline production at the refinery after the incident. In contrast, the ExxonMobil incident resulted in the shutdown of a very large part of the plant, essentially halting production of gasoline for a prolonged period. The Chevron incident allowed parts of the refinery to operate at significantly higher expense using feedstock brought in from elsewhere. Our analysis of the impact of these two incidents on gasoline prices indicates that the 2012 incident was somewhat less disruptive than the 2015 incident, though the two incidents are of similar magnitude and are both larger than other California incidents in the past decade. By analyzing changes in gasoline prices during the refinery incident (before Chevron was given permission to resume full production), we can develop a rough estimate of the lost production at the refinery. We estimate the total value of this lost production to be approximately $900 million. From this, we estimate the lost profit to the refiner to be $63 million for this incident. However, it is likely to be much larger than this number because this estimate does not include the higher cost of intermediate feedstock products that Chevron needed to import to the Richmond Refinery when the crude unit was off-line (i.e., the price of the feedstock over the price of crude).

---

[1] Private communication from Randall L. Sawyer, chief environmental health and hazardous material officer, Contra Costa Health Services, June 26, 2015.

[2] Private communication from Randall L. Sawyer, chief environmental health and hazardous material officer, Contra Costa Health Services, June 26, 2015.

Tosco Refinery Incident of 1999

The Tosco refinery incident could have easily been prevented. A tower fractionator system was leaking and was in need of repair. The CSB investigation into the cause of the incident determined that refinery workers should not have been asked to attempt to repair the leaking fractionator tower while it was in operation (CSB, 2001). The unit should have been shut down before repairs were attempted. However, a unit shutdown would have led to a reduction in gasoline production and sales revenue, so workers attempted to repair the unit while it was in full operation.

Repair and Worker-Safety Training Costs

Tosco did not provide a separate cost for refinery repairs for this incident. However, the refiner did provide a cost for refinery repairs and for the worker-safety training program that regulators called for as a result of the incident. The press reported the total cost for these at $41 million (Tansey, 2000).

Fines

Tosco was fined $3 million as result of the 1999 incident (Tansey, 2000).

Nearby Residents' Health Care Costs

A plume of hazardous gases resulted from the fire at the fractionation tower, which appeared to have some impact on the surrounding community. As a result of the incident, nearby residents initiated litigation against Tosco. We could not determine the adverse health effects that nearby residents suffered as a result of the incident or the resulting health care costs.

Emergency Response Costs

We could not ascertain the emergency response costs that fire and police departments incurred during the incident or how much of this cost Tosco might have paid.

Production Profit Losses

We can, however, estimate the losses from such incidents by looking at the value of the product that is not produced. In 1999, the Tosco refinery was rated at 110,000 bpd. The refinery was closed for five months as a result of the incident. If this incident were to occur today, it would have a major impact on the California gas market. At today's prices—say, $4 per gallon—its output for six months is worth about $2.8 billion. As described earlier in this report, a production loss of this magnitude qualifies this incident as a CMRI.

We use the same approach used in the ExxonMobil incident to estimate production profit losses. That is, we use 7 percent as a good estimate of actual economic loss to the refiner. In the Tosco case, this comes to $194 million for a five-month refinery outage.

Summary

We have estimated the costs of CMRIs to the refinery company suffering the incident. We considered the three costliest MRIs that have taken place in California in the past 16 years: the ExxonMobil Torrance incident of 2015, the Chevron Richmond incident of 2012, and the 1999 Tosco refinery incident. It is not possible for any of three incidents to present a definitive estimate of all refiner costs. Nevertheless, it is possible to estimate a lower bound for these costs.

We estimate that the cost of the Chevron Richmond Refinery incident of 2012 to Chevron was at least $80 million ($17 million plus $63 million) and might be significantly higher than this when the following costs (which we do not know) are included: all litigation resulting from the incident once settled, the additional costs of purchasing feedstock instead of crude oil, and all equipment repair costs.

We estimate the cost of the ExxonMobil Torrance Refinery incident of 2015 to ExxonMobil to be at least $323 million (for a six-month refinery outage). In this case, the cost might also be significantly higher than this when we include the additional costs of reconfiguring overseas refineries to produce California-grade reformulated gasoline, purchasing gasoline from overseas refineries, and transporting it to Torrance and of refinery equipment repair costs. Press reports indicate that ExxonMobil started importing some California-grade gasoline for the first time in June 2015 ("ExxonMobil Importing Asian Gasoline for the First Time Since LA-Area Refinery Explosion," 2015).

The cost of the Tosco refinery incident of 1999 to the refinery was at least $238 million. This includes fines, lost production profits, refinery-repair costs, and the costs of a worker training program that regulators ordered as a result of the incident. However, it does not include health care or ligation costs.

No two MRIs are exactly the same. Future incidents will also likely differ in important respects. The three CMRIs considered in this section provide a useful model for understanding the impact of costly major incidents. Such incidents are rare, and each is unique. Nevertheless, we can use these three incidents to get a rough sense of the costs of such incidents. On average, a costly major incident cost California refiners $220 million. This is a cost that could be avoided if the proposed regulations are implemented and do, as intended, improve refinery and worker safety.

It should also be noted that the loss to the refiner is not the same as the impact on the refinery industry as a whole in the state of California. In Chapter Five, we calculated that the supply shortage that the ExxonMobil Torrance Refinery incident caused resulted in a price increase of about $0.40 per gallon in the state of California. This happened without significant increases in the production costs for the other refiners. This resulted in a windfall profit on the order of $2.4 billion to the refiners that maintained or increased production during this time. Thus, although the losses to the refiner having the incident were significant, the gains for the rest of the industry were more than four times as great as those losses.

CHAPTER NINE

Balancing Costs and Benefits

To compare the costs and benefits of the regulations, we use a break-even analysis framework.

Analytical Approach

The specific break-even analysis approach we adopt is one that has been used in terrorism risk modeling and that can be applied to a broad set of cost–benefit problems (Willis and LaTourrette, 2008). We use this approach to estimate the critical risk-reduction factor, C_r, associated with changing regulations from their current form to the proposed regulations (C_r is defined in Chapter Three).

As shown in Chapter Five, the ExxonMobil Torrance 2015, Chevron Richmond 2012, and Tosco 1999 incidents appear to be the costliest major incidents that have occurred in California in the past 20 years. As explained in Chapter Five, less costly major incidents are more frequent than major incidents that result in major costs for California consumers, complicating an analysis of this sort. We focus on those very costly major incidents because they are responsible for the vast majority of the economic losses resulting from refinery incidents.

It should be observed that incidents of this magnitude are rare—only three such incidents have occurred in the past two decades in the state of California. Consequently, the variance for this data set is large, which indicates significant uncertainty associated with the estimates for annual loss from such events. In light of this uncertainty, we can generalize the analysis to account for a range of estimates for the true expected cost of major refinery events in the state of California. Figure 9.1 shows the relationship between estimated preregulation annual expected loss from major refinery events and the critical risk reduction required to justify the expense of the proposed regulations. Larger expected annual loss assumptions require smaller reductions in risk in order for the benefits of regulation to offset the costs, while lower estimates of expected annual loss (because, for example, of lower estimates of refinery incident frequency) must produce greater improvements in risk to be worthwhile. Figure 9.2

Figure 9.1
Critical Risk Reduction as a Function of Differing Estimates of Preregulation Expected Annual Loss from Costly Major Refinery Incidents

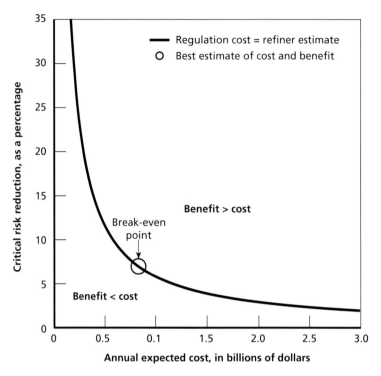

RAND *RR1421-9.1*

shows the same risk-reduction curve but places it in the context of the high and low cost scenarios examined earlier (refiner estimated, low cost, and high cost).

As described above, the small circle in Figure 9.1 indicates our best estimate for the break-even point.

Table 9.1 shows a small subset of possible points from Figure 9.2 to illustrate how several key factors are related in these uncertainty calculations. Given our best estimate of the cost of the regulations (developed in conjunction with California refiners) and our best estimate of expected loss from major incidents (based on the estimated cost of recent incidents), we calculate that the regulations must reduce risk by at least 7.3 percent in order to break even and be worth their cost. Under the low-cost scenario (for regulation implementation costs), risk must be reduced by only 2.5 percent, whereas under the high-cost scenario, risk must be reduced by 22.9 percent to justify the cost of the regulations. If one assumes an expected annual loss from costly major refinery incidents of only $400 million, these critical risk-reduction values rise, with the refiner-estimated costs requiring a reduction of 14.5 percent, the low-cost scenario 5 percent, and the high-cost scenario 45.9 percent. If, on the other hand, one assumes

Figure 9.2
Effect That Uncertainty About Regulation Cost Has on Critical
Risk-Reduction Value

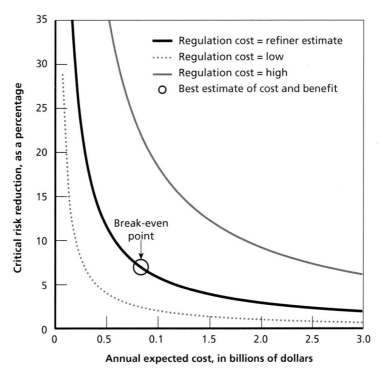

RAND *RR1421-9.2*

Table 9.1
Critical Risk-Reduction Values for Various Assumptions Regarding Expected
Annual Loss and Regulation Cost

Expected Annual Loss, in Millions of Dollars	Critical Risk Reduction, as a Percentage		
	Low Estimate of Implementation Costs	Refiner-Estimated Implementation Costs	High Estimate of Implementation Costs
200	10.0	29.0	91.7
400	5.0	14.5	45.9
800[a]	2.5	7.3[b]	22.9
1,200	1.7	4.8	15.3
1,600	1.3	3.6	11.5

[a] Best estimate of expected annual loss.

[b] Best estimate of break-even point.

an expected annual cost of $1.2 billion, the critical risk-reduction values are 4.8 percent in the refiner-estimated case, 1.7 percent in the low-cost case, and 15.3 percent in the high-cost case.

Our analysis of ISO versus NISO refineries in the previous chapter supports the idea that more-stringent regulation can produce real gains in refinery safety. To the extent that the proposed regulations resemble the Contra Costa County ISO, we might expect similar improvements. To the extent that the proposed regulations go beyond the ISO, they might be expected to produce greater safety gains—though various differences in the structure and implementation of the two regulatory regimes make precise quantitative comparison difficult.

Under most scenarios examined in this analysis, the regulations appear to be cost-effective. The various cells in Table 9.1 do not have equal probability. Our best estimate for expected loss from MRIs is $800 million per year, and our best estimate for the cost of the regulations (developed from refiner surveys) is $58 million per year. These most likely estimates require the regulations to reduce risk by 7.3 percent in order to be economically justified. This seems quite attainable given the success of the Contra Costa County ISO. If annual losses are actually lower, or if the cost of the regulations will actually be higher, the case for the regulations is less strong. In particular, if the annual losses are in the range of $200 million per year (one-quarter of what we have estimated), the critical risk reduction approaches 30 percent under the refiner-estimated cost scenario. Similarly, if regulatory implementation costs resemble the high end of the refiner estimates, the required risk reductions climb to more than 25 percent if annual losses are anything less than we have estimated.

On the other hand, most of the refiner-estimated cost scenarios appear justifiable. If annual losses are more than half of what we have estimated (more than $400 million per year), risk reductions of less than 15 percent are required to justify the regulations. Similarly, if the costs of implementation are closer to the low end of the refiner estimates, no plausible expected loss scenario requires a risk reduction of more than 10 percent. Even under the high-cost scenario, expected losses at or above our best estimate of $800 million per year require risk reductions of less than 25 percent. Reductions of this magnitude seem quite plausible given the history of the Contra Costa County ISO.

Our estimate for expected annual losses is conservative. We omit losses from all but the three most major recent incidents. Also, we have based our cost for the ExxonMobil incident on a shutdown time of six months. Estimates as of this writing are that the refinery might be off-line for a full 12 months. This might lead to a significant increase in the estimate for expected annual losses. If so, this would drive the critical risk-reduction levels downward, making the regulations more cost-effective.

Important Qualitative Factors

This analysis was able to capture and quantify most of the potential costs of the regulation but was less able to quantify benefits, such as avoided injury, avoided environmental harm, and peace of mind for the people of California. To the extent that this statement is true, the numbers presented here provide a conservative estimate of the benefits. This has the effect of lowering the required break-even point and making the regulations easier to justify.

CHAPTER TEN

Conclusions

The objective of this study was to assess the costs and benefits of the proposed California PSM and CalARP regulations that are designed to improve the safety of oil and gas refineries operating in the state of California.

These costs and benefits fall into four categories:

- costs to industry (to implement the regulation)
- costs to society (pass-through of certain industry costs)
- benefits to industry (costs avoided)
- benefits to society (costs avoided and other improvements and fewer worker deaths).

Costs to Industry

We engaged process safety and cost experts at each refinery to develop comprehensive estimates of the costs to implement all aspects of the proposed regulation. We provide the details of these cost estimates in Chapter Four and summarize them below.

There were significant differences in the size and composition of the proprietary cost estimates we received from the 12 refiners that operate in the state. We employed several cost-aggregation techniques to handle these differences and to account for capacity differences between refineries. Summing costs from all refiners produced a best estimate of $58 million per year for refiners to maintain compliance with the proposed regulations. Using the aggregation techniques described in Chapter Four, we calculate a range of $20 million per year on the low end and $183 million per year on the high end (see Table 10.1).

We base these estimates on detailed answers that refiners provided to a set of structured interview questions designed as part of the study to elicit the expected marginal costs of the proposed regulations over various aspects of PSM.

In most cases, refiners provided comprehensive answers for expected ongoing costs. We took the refiner-provided numbers at face value as good-faith estimates of the cost of compliance. These costs were reasonably consistent with one another, a fact

75

Table 10.1
Estimated Marginal Cost of
Regulatory Compliance, in Dollars

Estimate	Amount
Refiner-estimated total	57,571,983
Low	19,589,755
High	183,420,000

that built some confidence in the estimates. We used the variation in the estimates to construct the range of estimates by calculating a size-adjusted cost for each refiner and then taking the 10th percentile (second-lowest) and 90th percentile (second-highest) estimates as the likely lower and upper bounds for the unit cost of compliance. We then applied these unit costs to all refiners to develop the published ranges.

The one area of significant disagreement in the refiner cost estimates is start-up costs. Most refiners estimated start-up costs for the first one to five years to be on the same order as, or lower than, ongoing costs. One refining company, however, expressed concern about the costs to comply with SPA and LOPA provisions of the proposed regulation. They estimated that compliance with these provisions would require immediate or nearly immediate implementation of all SPA and LOPA recommendations that were feasible. In addition, they interpreted *feasible* to mean that the refinery would have to implement all recommended safeguards that were technically feasible regardless of cost. This interpretation of the proposed regulation would greatly increase the cost of compliance. If this refiner's assessment of the proposed regulation is correct, costs in the first five years could be 20 times as high as our estimate of ongoing costs. We did not include these SPA and LOPA start-up costs in the core cost estimates presented in Table 10.1. Informed by our own independent reading of the proposed regulation, we conclude that the other ten refiners have properly interpreted the proposed regulation.

Costs to Society

We have estimated the price impact of the proposed regulations under the assumptions that additional regulatory costs will be passed on to consumers through increased gasoline prices and that demand for gasoline is perfectly inelastic. In recent years, gasoline consumption in California has averaged about 14.5 billion gallons per year. Spreading the $58 million estimated cost of the regulations across this volume of sales indicates an increase in price of about $0.004 per gallon. The lower estimate of $20 million moves this impact down to $0.0014, while the upper estimate of $183 million moves the impact up to $0.013 per gallon.

Aggregating this up to calculate the impact on the average adult Californian gives an estimated cost per person of about $2 per year, with a low estimate of $0.68 and a high estimate of $6.20 per person per year. Consequently, we surmise that the impact that the proposed regulations would have on most California consumers would be modest.

Benefits to Industry

Costs Avoided

Safety improvements might result from implementing the proposed regulation. These safety improvements could reduce the number of CMRIs. Therefore, a benefit to industry of the proposed regulation is that the costs of major incidents could be avoided in the future. Below, we estimate the costs of a major incident for a California refinery that suffers the incident.

Refiners that suffer major incidents will incur the types of costs listed here:

- equipment repair costs
- workers' compensation
- fines
- nearby residents' health care costs
- emergency response costs
- lost profit from reduced production.

Our analysis reveals that the average cost of CMRIs that have occurred in the past 16 years is at least $220 million.

Caveats

This cost estimate does not include the costs of

- all refinery equipment repairs
- liability claims
- personal-injury claims
- gross-negligence claims
- reputation damage
- retooling and reconfiguration of overseas refineries to produce California-grade reformulated gasoline
- overseas manufacturing and transportation of California blend gasoline
- purchase and transportation of intermediate process gasoline feedstock.

We could not independently estimate the above costs without access to proprietary information that refiners hold.

Safety Improvements

Safety improvements might result from implementing the proposed regulation. These safety improvements could reduce the number of MRIs. The analysis of ISO and NISO MRI histories presented in this report provides support for this hypothesis. In this analysis, we showed that the incident rate for major incidents was much less for ISO refineries, as indicated in Table 10.2.

Statistical Significance and Other Factors

In Chapter Five, we showed that the NISO probability has a relatively narrow CI, and the ISO-refinery data population is distinct from the NISO distribution. However, there are not enough data points in the ISO sample to say that the quantitative difference between the two probabilities is statistically significant. Nevertheless, we can say that the ISO refinery major incident rate is likely lower than that for NISO refineries.

The Contra Costa County ISO is a more stringent regulation than the current California or federal standard and contains some of the key elements of the proposed refinery regulations. In fact, the proposed regulations build on the ISO requirement, requiring state-of-the-art PSM practices that are designed to provide greater levels of reliability and safety than the Contra Costa County ISO currently provides. Therefore, it is not unreasonable to assume that California refinery-incident rates under the proposed regulation will be similar to, or lower than, those of ISO refineries. Refiners that implement the measures called for in the proposed regulation should suffer fewer major incidents and thereby avoid many of the ensuing costs.

Given the above data, the reduced major incident rate for refineries operating under the proposed regulation will also likely lead to

- improved reliability of systems
- reduction in certain workers' compensation premiums
- improved community relations
- improved labor–management relations
- company reputation or public image improvements.

We found no evidence that the proposed regulations would reduce the long-term operating costs of California refineries, however.

Table 10.2
California Refinery Major Incident Rates

Refinery Type	Annual Major Incident Rate, as a Percentage
ISO	0
NISO	6.6

Benefits to Society

Costs Avoided

In quantitative terms, the largest potential benefit of the proposed regulations is the avoided cost of fuel-supply disruption related to a future MRI. Our analysis of gasoline prices in California versus the rest of the United States in response to the 2014 Exxon-Mobil Torrance incident indicated a cost to California drivers of nearly $2.4 billion, which took the form of a prolonged $0.40 increase in gasoline prices. Macroeconomic analysis indicates that the lost supply associated with this one incident reduced the size of the California economy by $6.9 billion. Similar analysis of the Chevron Richmond 2012 and Tosco 1999 incidents indicated costs to the California economy of $1.7 billion and $4.1 billion, respectively, though it should be noted that the Tosco estimate is based on the current structure of the California economy and gasoline market, rather than on conditions in 1999.

The estimated costs to California consumers and to the California economy for the ExxonMobil 2015 incident assume a refinery outage of six months in duration. Press reports now indicate that the ExxonMobil Torrance refinery outage might last up to 12 months. In this case, the costs above to California consumers and to the California economy would double.

Having fewer refinery incidents enables Californians to avoid other costs that residents would incur who live near the refinery afflicted by the incident. These include costs for

- emergency services
- health care
- reduction in property values
- reduction in local tax revenue to local governments.

Deaths Avoided

A reduction in MRIs should confer other noneconomic benefits on residents living near refineries. They would be less likely to be injured or die in such incidents. However, we could not quantify this noneconomic benefit for residents in this study.

A reduction in MRIs also would confer noneconomic benefits on refinery workers. They would be less likely to be injured or die in such incidents.

If such events can be avoided, worker safety will be improved, and the number of workers who die will be reduced. In this study, we examined the hypothesis that the implementation of the proposed regulation will in fewer refinery-worker deaths. We examined worker deaths in ISO and NISO refineries and find that these data provide statistically significant evidence to support this hypothesis.

Table 10.3 summarizes our analysis of refinery-worker death rates.

Table 10.3
California Refinery-Worker Death Rates

Refinery Type	Annual Worker Death Rate, as a Percentage
ISO	0
NISO	7.0

Statistical Significance

In this analysis, we showed that the ISO refinery-worker death rate was much less than the worker death rate for NISO refineries operating in the state of California. In Chapter Five, we showed that the quantitative difference in worker death rate is not statistically significant; however, we can say that the ISO refinery-worker death rate is likely lower than that for NISO refineries.

Balancing Costs and Benefits

To compare the costs and benefits of the regulations, we have used a break-even analysis framework. The analysis presented here leads us to conclude that the regulations need to make California refineries 7.3 percent safer than they are under the current regulations in order to be worth their cost (based on the best estimates of the refiners for regulation implementation costs and our best estimate for expected loss from MRIs, i.e., $800 million per year). The analysis of incidents under both the ISO and NISO regulatory regimes presented in Chapter Eight supports the idea that safety gains of at least this magnitude are possible.

It should also be noted that this analysis has been able to capture and quantify most of the potential costs of the regulation but has been less able to quantify benefits, such as avoided injury, avoided environmental harm, and peace of mind for the people of California. To the extent that this statement is true, the numbers presented here provide a conservative estimate of the benefits. This has the effect of lowering the required break-even point and making the regulations easier to justify.

Structured Interview Questions

In this appendix, we reproduce the questions we used in our structured interviews.

RAND Refinery Regulation Study
Structured Interview Questions
May 2015

General
The State of California is proposing changes to process safety management (PSM) and Accidental Release Prevention Program (CalARP) regulations at petroleum refineries.

In qualitative terms, how many additional resources do you think your company will need to meet the new PSM regulatory requirements?

Please indicate the answer that best describes your refinery's situation.
1. No additional resources required. We are meeting virtually all of the requirements already.
2. Marginal additional resources required. We are doing the many of the things required, but will need to adjust them somewhat and/or report them differently.
3. Significant additional resources required. We will need to hire people, buy equipment, redesign processes, etc. in order to meet the proposed regulatory requirements.
4. Major additional resources required. We will have to make big changes and completely rethink our safety regime.

Does your refinery break out PSM/CalARP costs from other refinery operations or production costs?

If you break out this cost, about how much do you spend annually on complying with these regulations today?

If your refinery is in Contra Costa County, about how much do you spend on complying with the ISO annually?

About how much do you expect the proposed regulations will add to the refinery's cost of operation or to your current PSM compliance costs?

How confident are you in the cost estimates given in response to the prior questions?

Please indicate the answer that describes your confidence level.
1. Not very confident
2. Somewhat confident. Significant uncertainty regarding this cost.
3. Confident. Informed estimate.
4. Very confident. Data-driven analysis.

Do you expect the regulations to result in significant safety improvements (better reliability, fewer fires, few explosions, fewer hazardous material releases and reduced accident rates or workplace injuries)?

Refinery Size
These questions provide some basic context on the scale of your refinery.

What is the capacity of your refinery as measured in terms of barrels per day?

How many people does the refinery typically employ?
- Regular employees
- Contractors

As a first order measure of the complexity of the infrastructure, can you estimate the total length of pipe (of all kinds) in the refinery?

If you have calculated it, what is the Nelson Complexity Index of your refinery?

Safety Training
The new regulations require a well-documented program of training on safety and health hazards, emergency operations including shutdown, and safe work practices applicable to employees job tasks. It further requires that this training be refreshed every three years.

Do you expect the proposed regulations to prompt significant changes in your training programs? If so, please describe the nature and estimated cost of the changes.

Damage Mechanism Reviews
The proposed regulations require refineries to conduct a damage mechanism review (DMR) for all covered processes. They require this review to be revalidated every five years. The regulations further require operators to prepare a report on the DMR and review it with all personnel whose work assignments are within the scope of the DMR.

Do you currently do DMRs?

Do you currently do DMRs for all processes covered in the proposed regulations or just for a subset?

About how many DMRs do you currently do each year?

Can you estimate the costs of current DMRs, in terms of personnel and other costs?

Given your current understanding of the proposed requirements, how many additional DMRs would you estimate doing under these regulations?

Please provide program cost estimates for a single typical DMR, broken out by staffing costs, contractor costs, and other costs.

If your facility currently does DMRs, please describe typical actions that follow DMR recommendations.

Please estimate costs associated with these typical actions (e.g., increased inspection frequency, repairs, replacement/infrastructure costs).

Would your procedures for doing DMRs change under the new requirements?

Would the typical actions that follow DMR recommendations change under the new requirements? Please describe the costs associated with these changes.

Please estimate any cost savings associated with the DMR process and the actions that follow the recommendations.

How much of the cost above is one-time upfront cost to meet the regulations?

How much is recurring annual cost?

If possible, please provide a brief description of the kinds of costs in each of these categories (upfront and recurring), particularly with respect to the categories of personnel, consultant services, and other.

Root Cause Analysis

The proposed regulations require refineries to conduct a root cause analysis (RCA) for all incidents that result or could reasonably have resulted in a major incident. The regulations further require operators to submit a report on the incident investigation (for major incidents only) to the UPA for public posting.

Do you currently do RCAs? For what type of incidents or events?

Do you currently do RCAs for all incidents covered in the proposed regulations?

About how many RCAs do you currently do each year (taking the past three years as representative)?

Can you estimate the total annual costs of current RCAs, in terms of personnel and other costs?

Given your current understanding of the proposed requirements, how many additional RCAs would you estimate doing under these regulations?

Please provide program cost estimates for a single RCA, broken out by staffing costs, contractor costs, and other costs.

If your facility currently does RCAs, please describe typical actions that follow RCA recommendations.

Please estimate costs associated with these typical actions (e.g., increased inspection frequency, repairs, replacement/infrastructure costs).

Would your procedures for doing RCAs change under the new requirements?

Would the typical actions that follow RCA recommendations change under the new requirements? Please describe the costs associated with these changes.

Please estimate any cost savings associated with the RCA process and the actions that follow the recommendations.

How much of the cost above is one-time upfront cost to meet the regulations?

How much is recurring annual cost?

If possible, please provide a brief description of the kinds of costs in each of these categories (upfront and recurring), particularly with respect to the categories of personnel, consultant services, and other.

Hierarchy of Hazard Control Analysis

The proposed regulations require refineries to conduct a hierarchy of control analysis (HCA) under various circumstances and to produce an HCA report. HCA is also sometimes referred to as Inherently Safer Systems/Designs (ISS/D). The HCA report must contain a description of the hazards, potential prevention and control measures, a description of the method used, the findings, recommendations and conclusions, the rationale for the conclusions, the timeline to address the findings, and the plan to communicate the findings. Employee representatives must be included in every aspect of the HCA.

Refineries will be required to conduct an HCA prior to the next Process Hazard Analysis (PHA) and to update it every 5 years to reduce process safety risks to the greatest extent feasible. The regulations further require operators to conduct an HCA under the following circumstances:
- Whenever a PHA results in a recommended action item.

- **Whenever a major change is proposed as part of a Management of Change (MOC) process.**
- **Whenever a new process, process unit, or facility is designed and reviewed.**
- **Whenever an incident investigation produces recommended actions.**

Do you currently do HCAs (or ISS/D analyses)? Does this take the form of a written program?

Do you currently do HCAs in all of the circumstances covered in the proposed regulations or just for a subset?

Are HCAs incorporated into the PHA, Root Cause Analysis, or Mechanical Integrity program?

About how many HCAs do you currently do each year?

Can you estimate the total annual costs of current HCAs, in terms of personnel and other costs?

Given your current understanding of the proposed requirements, how many additional HCAs would you estimate doing under these regulations?

Please provide program cost estimates for a single HCA, broken out by staffing costs, contractor costs, equipment costs, and other costs.

If your facility currently does HCAs, please describe typical actions that follow HCA recommendations.

Please estimate costs associated with these typical actions (e.g., increased inspection frequency, repairs, replacement/infrastructure costs).

Would your procedures for doing HCAs change under the new requirements?

Would the typical actions that follow HCA recommendations change under the new requirements? Please describe the costs associated with these changes.

Please estimate any cost savings associated with the HCA process and the actions that follow the recommendations.

How much of the cost above is one-time upfront cost to meet the regulations?

How much is recurring annual cost?

If possible, please provide a brief description of the kinds of costs in each of these categories (upfront and recurring), particularly with respect to the categories of personnel, consultant services, and other.

Process Safety Culture Assessment

The proposed regulations require refineries to conduct a process safety culture assessment (PSCA) every 3 years using one or more of the following:

- **Anonymous survey,**
- **Interviews by people outside the refinery**
- **Observation by people outside the refinery**
- **Focus groups led by people outside the refinery**
- **Some other approved method**

This assessment must result in a safety culture report and action plan that is communicated to employees. The regulations require that employees and their representatives participate in all aspects of the safety culture assessment, report, and action plan.

Do you currently do PSCAs?

Do you currently do PSCAs using methods and frequency that would comply with the proposed regulations?

How often are PSCAs done at your facility? What method is used?

Can you estimate the costs of current PSCAs, in terms of personnel and other costs?

Please provide program cost estimates for a single PSCA, broken out by staffing costs, contractor costs, and other costs.

If your facility currently does PSCAs, please describe typical actions that follow the production of a safety culture report and action plan.

Please estimate costs associated with these typical actions (e.g., increased training, restructuring of management systems or procedures).

Would your procedures for doing PSCAs change under the new requirements?

Would the typical actions that follow a PSCA report and action plan change under the new requirements? Please describe the costs associated with these changes.

Please estimate any cost savings associated with the PSCA process and the actions that follow from it.

How much of the cost above is one-time upfront cost to meet the regulations?

How much is recurring annual cost?

If possible, please provide a brief description of the kinds of costs in each of these categories (upfront and recurring), particularly with respect to the categories of personnel, consultant services, and other.

Program Management

The proposed regulations require refineries to review and revise process safety management system procedures every two years as appropriate. These would include the development and implementation of written procedures for ensuring effective exchange and tracking of safety, operational, and maintenance information. They would also state how findings of all prevention elements are communicated to employees and how employee participation is incorporated. Refineries would be required to maintain a current organizational chart, job descriptions, and annual safety performance goals for personnel with responsibility for managing each prevention element and to have a system in place that evaluates the effectiveness of program elements and includes performance metrics, goals, and objectives.

Do you currently use the program management approaches required by the proposed regulations?

If your current program management differs from what is required by the proposed regulations, please describe the ways in which your current program is similar and the ways in which it differs.

Can you estimate the costs of current program management, in terms of personnel and other costs?

Given your current understanding of the proposed requirements, how much more would you estimate spending on program management under these regulations? Please break these costs out by personnel, consulting, and other costs.

Please estimate any cost savings associated with the revised program management procedures.

How much of the cost above is one-time upfront cost to meet the regulations?

How much is recurring annual cost?

If possible, please provide a brief description of the kinds of costs in each of these categories (upfront and recurring), particularly with respect to the categories of personnel, consultant services, and other.

Performance Indicators

The proposed regulations require refineries to track and report certain performance indicators. These include:

- **All past due inspections for piping and pressure vessels.**
- **All past due PHA recommended actions and seismic recommended actions.**
- **All past due incident investigation recommended actions for API RP 570 Tier 1 and Tier 2 incidents.**
- **All API RP 570 Tier 1 and 2 incidents.**

Is this currently being done at your facility? (For example, does your company currently use API 754?)

Do you currently track all of the performance measures in the proposed regulations or just for a subset?

Do you currently report any or all of the measures tracked outside of your facility? If so, how similar is this reporting to what would be required under the proposed regulations?

Can you estimate the costs of current performance indicator tracking and reporting, in terms of personnel and other costs?

Given your current understanding of the proposed requirements, would your procedures for doing tracking performance measures change? If so, please estimate the additional costs that would be incurred in terms of personnel, consulting, and other costs.

Please estimate any cost savings associated with the new performance indicator tracking and reporting processes.

How much of the cost above is one-time upfront cost to meet the regulations?

How much is recurring annual cost?

If possible, please provide a brief description of the kinds of costs in each of these categories (upfront and recurring), particularly with respect to the categories of personnel, consultant services, and other.

Human Factors

The proposed regulations require refineries to develop a written human factors program with employee involvement to include human factors considerations in all ARP programs. They further require refineries to implement human factor controls on process equipment, including error proof mechanisms, automatic alerts, and automatic system shutdowns for

critical operational errors; to train employees and, where applicable, contract employees in the human factors program; to implement written procedures to manage organizational change and to conduct management of organizational change analyses before and after changes.

How familiar are you with the proposed Human Factors regulations?

Do you currently have a written human factors program?

If you have such a program, does it meet all of the requirements of the proposed regulations? If not, please describe how it differs.

Can you estimate the costs of your current human factors program, in terms of personnel and other costs?

Assuming that the October 2014 draft of the regulation were the requirement, how much additional human factors work (expressed in terms of cost) would you estimate doing under these regulations?

Would your procedures for assessing and managing human factors change under the new requirements?

Would the typical actions that follow human factors analysis change under the new requirements? Please describe the costs associated with these changes.

Please estimate any cost savings associated with the human factors process and the actions that follow the recommendations.

How much of the cost above is one-time upfront cost to meet the regulations?

How much is recurring annual cost?

If possible, please provide a brief description of the kinds of costs in each of these categories (upfront and recurring), particularly with respect to the categories of personnel, consultant services, and other.

Safeguard Protection Analysis

The proposed regulations require refineries to conduct a Layer of Protection Analysis (LOPA) or other safeguard protection analysis (SPA) and to revalidate this analysis every 5 years. This should include a written compilation of potential initiating causes that could lead to hazard scenarios and determine the initiating event frequency rate. It should also include a written compilation of independent protection layers (IPLs) that prevent initiating events and quantify the risk reduction obtainable by each IPL. The proposed regulations require the preparation of a written report and an implementation schedule for actions to be taken.

Do you currently do LOPAs? If not, do you currently do some other form of SPA?

Do you currently do SPAs in a way that would meet the requirements of the proposed regulations?

Do you currently revalidate your SPA every 5 years? If not, is there a formal schedule for revalidation of SPAs?

Can you estimate the annual costs of your current SPA procedure, in terms of personnel and other costs?

Given your current understanding of the proposed requirements, how much additional SPA work (expressed in terms of cost) would you estimate doing under these regulations?

If your facility currently does SPAs, please describe typical actions that follow SPA recommendations.

Would your procedures for doing SPAs change under the new requirements?

Please estimate any cost savings associated with the revised SPA process and the actions that follow the recommendations.

How much of the cost above is one-time upfront cost to meet the regulations?

How much is recurring annual cost?

If possible, please provide a brief description of the kinds of costs in each of these categories (upfront and recurring), particularly with respect to the categories of personnel, consultant services, and other.

Unplanned Downtime

Please provide information on unplanned downtime incidents that your refinery has experienced over the past ten years. The information requested here is similar to that reported in the Solomon Survey.

Please note the scale (in percent of capacity terms) and duration of periods of unplanned downtime in the past ten years that have impacted more than 10% of production capacity for five days or more. Please provide the length of these downtime periods (in approximate number of days) and the approximate percentage of total refinery capacity lost in each incident. If the unplanned downtime is due to a power outage caused by an external utility provider please include but specify. If there are other unplanned downtimes that occur due to other external factors please specify.

PHA

The Process Hazard Analysis (PHA) is a critical component of PSM regulations. The proposed regulations may alter some of the circumstances where PHAs are required.

Are there any new initial PHAs that you would have to perform under the proposed regulations?

What are the costs associated with conducting the new PHAs and implementing the recommendations resulting from the new PHAs?

Are there any new seismic assessments you would have to perform under the proposed regulation?

What actions typically result from a seismic assessment?

What are the costs of a seismic assessment and typical recommendations that result from a seismic assessment?

RAGAGEP and Mechanical Integrity (MI)

The proposed regulations require that refineries document that process equipment complies with recognized and generally accepted good engineering practices (RAGAGEP) where RAGAGEP has been established for that process equipment, _or_ with internal standards and codes that ensure safe operation.

Does your current MI program meet the requirements of the proposed regulation?

Will your current MI program require any changes to meet the requirements of the proposed regulation?

Do you have a process for evaluating new or updated codes and standards and implementing (internal or external) RAGAGEP changes?

Can you estimate the costs of changes to your (internal or external) RAGAGEP and/or MI program?

Final Thoughts

Thanks for taking the time to discuss the proposed regulations in such detail. Having been through all of this detail, how confident are you in the numbers and/or characterizations that you have provided? Which of the following statements best characterizes the answers you have given?

Please indicate the answer that describes your confidence level.
1. Not very confident.

2. Somewhat confident. Significant uncertainty regarding this cost.
3. Confident. Informed estimate.
4. Very confident. Data-driven analysis.

Bibliography

American Petroleum Institute, "Process Safety Performance Indicators for the Refining and Petrochemical Industries," 1st ed., Recommended Practice 754, April 1, 2010.

API—*See* American Petroleum Institute.

Cagle, Susie, "A Year After a Refinery Explosion, Richmond, Calif., Is Fighting Back," *Grist*, August 6, 2013. As of January 19, 2016: http://grist.org/climate-energy/a-year-after-a-refinery-explosion-richmond-cali-is-fighting-back/

Caldwell, Jessica, "Drive by Numbers: Tesla in All 50 States," *Edmunds.com*, January 29, 2014. As of January 19, 2016: http://www.edmunds.com/industry-center/analysis/drive-by-numbers-tesla-in-all-50-states.html

CalEPA—*See* California Environmental Protection Agency.

California Code of Regulations, Title 8, Industrial Relations, Division 1, Department of Industrial Relations, Chapter 4, Division of Industrial Safety, Subchapter 7, General Industry Safety Orders, Group 16, Control of Hazardous Substances, Article 109, Hazardous Substances and Practices, Section 5189, Process Safety Management of Acutely Hazardous Materials. As of January 20, 2016: https://govt.westlaw.com/calregs/Document/I84760480DEE911E3AC39E1C90EDC1D02?viewType =FullText&originationContext=documenttoc&transitionType=CategoryPageItem&contextData=(sc. Default)

California Department of Finance, "Major Regulations," undated. As of August 9, 2015: http://www.dof.ca.gov/research/economic_research_unit/SB617_regulation/view.php

California Department of Motor Vehicles, "State of California Department of Motor Vehicles Statistics for Publication January Through December 2014," March 2015. As of August 8, 2015: https://www.dmv.ca.gov/portal/wcm/connect/5aa16cd3-39a5-402f-9453-0d353706cc9a/official. pdf?MOD=AJPERES

California Environmental Protection Agency, "California Reformulated Gasoline Phase 3 (CaRFG3)," page last updated July 24, 2015. As of August 9, 2015: http://www.arb.ca.gov/fuels/gasoline/carfg3/carfg3.htm

California Senate, State Government: Financial and Administrative Accountability, Senate Bill 617, chaptered October 6, 2011. As of January 20, 2016: http://leginfo.legislature.ca.gov/faces/billStatusClient.xhtml?bill_id=201120120SB617

Cal/OSHA—*See* Division of Occupational Safety and Health.

Center for Effective Government, "The Right-to-Know Network," undated. As of January 22, 2016: http://www.rtknet.org/

Chevron USA, Richmond Refinery Site Safety Plan, February 2013.

Chevron USA Richmond Investigation Team, "Richmond Refinery 4 Crude Unit Incident, August 6, 2012," April 12, 2013. As of January 19, 2016:
http://richmond.chevron.com/Files/richmond/Investigation_Report.pdf

City of Richmond, California, *An Ordinance of the City Council of the City of Richmond Amending Chapter 6.43 of the Richmond Municipal Code Relating to Industrial Safety*, Ordinance 1-13 N.S., February 5, 2013. As of January 19, 2016:
http://www.ci.richmond.ca.us/ArchiveCenter/ViewFile/Item/4988

Contra Costa Health Services, "Major Accidents at Chemical/Refinery Plants in Contra Costa County," undated. As of January 22, 2016:
http://cchealth.org/hazmat/accident-history.php

———, *Hazardous Materials Incident Notification Policy*, December 14, 2004; revised February 2010. As of January 19, 2016:
http://cchealth.org/hazmat/pdf/incident_notification_policy.pdf

———, *Annual Review and Evaluation Report 2014: Industrial Safety Ordinance—ISO Report*, December 9, 2014. As of January 19, 2016:
http://cchealth.org/hazmat/pdf/iso/iso-report.pdf

Contra Costa Health Services Hazardous Materials Program, *Industrial Safety Ordinance: City of Richmond Annual Performance Review and Evaluation Report*, July 26, 2011. As of January 19, 2016:
http://cchealth.org/hazmat/pdf/iso/iso_report_richmond.pdf

CSB—*See* U.S. Chemical Safety and Hazard Investigation Board.

Division of Occupational Safety and Health, Department of Industrial Relations, State of California, *Proposed GISO* §5189.1, version 4.5, May 26, 2015. As of January 20, 2016:
http://www.dir.ca.gov/dosh/DoshReg/Process-Safety-Management-for-Refineries/PSM-Draft-Regulation.2015-05-26.pdf

"ExxonMobil Importing Asian Gasoline for the First Time Since LA-Area Refinery Explosion," *Platts*, June 18, 2015. As of August 15, 2015:
http://www.platts.com/latest-news/shipping/houston/exxonmobil-importing-asian-gasoline-for-the-first-21642766

Hopkins, Andrew, "The Cost–Benefit Hurdle for Safety Case Regulation," *Safety Science*, Vol. 77, August 2015, pp. 95–101.

IMPLAN Group, home page, undated. As of January 20, 2016:
http://www.implan.com/

Interagency Working Group on Refinery Safety, *Improving Public and Worker Safety at Oil Refineries: Draft Report of the Interagency Working Group on Refinery Safety*, July 2013. As of January 19, 2016:
http://citeseerx.ist.psu.edu/viewdoc/download?doi=10.1.1.396.5925&rep=rep1&type=pdf

Leontief, Wassily, *The Structure of American Economy, 1919–1929: An Empirical Application of Equilibrium Analysis*, Cambridge, Mass.: Harvard University Press, 1941.

———, *Studies in the Structure of the American Economy: Theoretical and Empirical Explorations in Input–Output Analysis*, New York: Oxford University Press, 1953.

Malewitz, Jim, Mark Collette, and Lise Olsen, "Anatomy of Disaster: Studies Pinpointed What Went Wrong in Texas City, but Unsafe Conditions Persist," *Texas Tribune*, March 22, 2015. As of January 19, 2016:
http://apps.texastribune.org/blood-lessons/disaster/

Penn, Ivan, "Exxon Mobil Scraps Plans for Temporary Fix to Damaged Torrance Refinery," *Los Angeles Times*, September 23, 2015. As of January 19, 2016:
http://www.latimes.com/business/la-fi-exxon-refinery-plans-20150923-story.html

Rocha, Veronica, "Too Much Pressure in Equipment Triggered Torrance Refinery Explosion," *Los Angeles Times*, February 23, 2015a. As of August 14, 2015:
http://www.latimes.com/local/lanow/la-me-ln-exxon-mobil-refinery-blast-20150223-story.html

———, "Exxon Mobil Fined $566,600 for Torrance Refinery Explosion," *Los Angeles Times*, August 13, 2015b. As of January 19, 2016:
http://www.latimes.com/local/lanow/la-me-ln-exxon-mobil-refinery-explosion-20150813-story.html

Rosner, Bernard, *Fundamentals of Biostatistics*, Cengage Learning, 2015.

Sawyer, Randall L., chief environmental health and hazardous-material officer, Contra Costa Health Services, "Written Testimony of Randall L. Sawyer," hearing on "Oversight of Federal Risk Management and Emergency Planning Programs to Prevent and Address Chemical Threats, Including the Events Leading Up to the Explosions in West, TX and Geismar, LA," before the Committee on Environment and Public Works, U.S. Senate, June 27, 2013. As of January 19, 2016:
http://www.epw.senate.gov/public/_cache/files/0e37eb9e-8f43-47a7-ae82-de172eb414cb/62713hearingwitnesstestimonysawyer.pdf

Shell Martinez Refinery, *RAND Pre-Publication Draft Copy: "Cost Benefit Analysis of Proposed CA Oil and Gas Refinery Regulations"—Shell Martinez Refinery Comments on References to Shell*, private correspondence, February 1, 2016, not available to the general public.

Sider, Alison, "PBF to Buy Southern California Refinery from Exxon for $537.5 Million," *Wall Street Journal*, September 30, 2015. As of January 19, 2016:
http://www.wsj.com/articles/pbf-to-buy-southern-california-refinery-from-exxon-for-537-5-million-1443646641

Sunstein, Cass R., *Risk and Reason: Safety, Law, and Environment*, Cambridge, UK: Cambridge University Press, 2004.

Tansey, Bernadette, "Explosion at Tosco: One Year Later—Uneasy in Fire's Aftermath: Contra Costa Officials Wonder If a Refinery Can Be Made Safe," *SFGate*, February 21, 2000. As of January 19, 2016:
http://www.sfgate.com/bayarea/article/EXPLOSION-AT-TOSCO-ONE-YEAR-LATER-Uneasy-in-3304729.php

Tesoro Refining and Marketing, *Response to "Cost Benefit Analysis of Proposed California Oil and Gas Refinery Regulations,"* private communication, January 22, 2016, not available to the general public.

U.S. Chemical Safety and Hazard Investigation Board, *Investigation Report: Refinery Fire Incident*, Report 99-014-I-CA, March 21, 2001. As of January 19, 2016:
http://www.csb.gov/tosco-avon-refinery-petroleum-naphtha-fire/

———, *Interim Investigation Report: Chevron Richmond Refinery Fire*, April 2013. As of January 19, 2016:
http://www.csb.gov/assets/1/19/Chevron_Interim_Report_Final_2013-04-17.pdf

———, *Regulatory Report: Chevron Richmond Refinery Pipe Rupture and Fire*, Report 2012-03-I-CA, May 2014. As of January 19, 2016:
http://www.csb.gov/assets/1/19/Chevron_Regulatory_Report_06272014.pdf

———, *Final Investigation Report: Chevron Richmond Refinery Pipe Rupture and Fire*, Report 2012-03-I-CA, January 2015. As of January 19, 2016:
http://www.csb.gov/assets/1/19/Chevron_Final_Investigation_Report_2015-01-28.pdf

Western States Petroleum Association, *Economic Contributions of the Petroleum Industry in California's Oil Producing and Refining Regions: Southern California, Central Coast, San Joaquin Valley, San Francisco Bay Area*, Sacramento, Calif., undated. As of February 10, 2016:
https://www.wspa.org/sites/default/files/uploads/documents/
Petroleum%20Industry%20Economic%20Impacts%20-%20California.pdf

Willis, Henry H., and Tom LaTourrette, "Using Probabilistic Terrorism Risk Modeling for Regulatory Benefit–Cost Analysis: Application to the Western Hemisphere Travel Initiative Implemented in the Land Environment," *Risk Analysis*, Vol. 28, No. 2, April 2008, pp. 325–339.